Frank, thanks for your friendship and faithfulness to the Lord, keep the faith brother.

LIVING IN THE *HEAT* OF THE BATTLE

The Incredible Journey of men Caught in a Marriage gone Bad

WILLARD R. SIMMONS

xulon PRESS

Living in the Heat of the Battle
The Incredible Journey of men Caught in a Marriage gone Bad
by Willard R. Simmons

Printed in the United States of America

ISBN 978-1-60647-071-8

www.xulonpress.com

Contents

APPENDIX

INTRODUCTION

Understanding The Battle Grounds

"You're so useless and never do anything around the house. I'm glad I'm not close to you. You're just a horrible person to be around. Why don't you just go away for the day so I don't have to see you"

These words were spoken by the wife of a friend of mine named Mike. As we sat together at the table over lunch, he had come to me crushed, depressed and tired of hiding his shameful marriage to others. For years he hid all his troubles by somehow pretending it would all get better. That his wife would repent and their marriage would turn around for the better. But as time and testing's moved forward, he grew tired and worn of the daily hardships, naggings and sharp, rude remarks from his wife. He had been married for over fifteen years and both he and his wife claimed to be Christians. They attended church together where he is a children's Sunday school teacher. Mike is a supervisor at a well-known Christian college and works very hard at his position. For the past several years his wife has become increasingly aggressive toward him both verbally and in the misuse of their money. Because of this he tried everything to avoid anything that would upset her. As he told me, *"When I get home it's like walking on glass around her. Almost anything I say or do offends her. I can't even have a descent conversation with her without it coming to an argument"* As time passed he found ways to stay longer at work or found things to do outside the house to stay away from his wife. Deep down inside he knew this was all wrong but he thought there was nothing more he could do to heal his marriage or to remove the dark cloud that seemed to hang over his life. He had tried to talk to her on several occasions but to no avail. All she would say is that it was his problem. Then she would go down a long list of things he was doing wrong. He could barely get a word in edge-wise. After several failures at trying to come up with a solution, he just through up his arms and said, *"I just give up. She won't listen anymore to common sense or reason. I don't know what to do."*

Over 30 years of counseling has shown me the amazing reality of how Christians can choose to live in this kind of marriage for many years without breaking the depressing daily grind of such tensions. I've actually lost count of all the men I knew who attended church, said they were Christians and had this kind of marriage. Everywhere I go I see this same thing. I have found the story about Mike a very common one among Christian men- more common than people might think. Looking around at church on Sunday morning at other couples, you may see smiling faces and what appears to be a good marriage. But people can be good actors. In reality many of these same couples are miserable. I did not realize this for many years until I started Biblical counseling and saw the tremendous overload of marital conflicts within the church, most hidden from the outward eye. There were so many marital problems that the counselors had a three-month waiting list of people who needed help. This awakened me to the reality that a lot of couples are very troubled and wished they could just get out of their marriages and find some sort of peace and tranquility, many eventually finding a pastor or counselor that would agree with their miserable situation and see themselves as a hopeless victim, granting them the so called "right of passage" to divorce, that God wants them happy. Most are shocked to find out that this problem is wide spread within the church.

I must admit that for many years I wasn't sure how to help men caught in this kind of situation. I know all the 1Timothy and Titus principles for men who desire and are called to be deacons or elders, but most men caught in this kind of marriage relationship just want some help to live day by day with their difficult wives. From what I've seen, when men do share their problems with others, what they usually find is little direction and hope. Most people tell them the common cliché, *"I'll pray for you."* Most pastors don't have a clue how to help them either. I know, I've seen it for years. When I survey the big picture of this huge problem within the church, what I see are three basic problems that keep feeding these terrible and sinful situations. The first is the lack of a solid biblical resource that actually gives men directions on how to please God and deal biblically with a wife like this. Second, the inability of church leadership to come along side men and help them as a brother. The third issue is at the core of this problem and that is the lack of true desire on the couple's part to truly repent and do things God's way-no matter the cost.

This book is not an attempt to help both the husband and wife as I would do in a counseling situation. It is designed for the man who finds himself in the situation like our friend Mike. Since there are a lot of books to help wives, I decided to write one for husbands.

God gives us all sound Biblical principles for how a man should respond to situations like this. He should never retreat or consider divorce. That's the easy way out and little will be gained by it. But if he strives to intently practice God's will in his situation, many good things will happen. Changes in his own character, thinking and spiritual walk will occur and he will be able to be steadfast through this long battle. I am convinced that anyone walking by the Spirit in obedience to God's Word can live with anyone. A well trained and hardened soldier is not this way unless he has succeeded in fighting many battles. Such a man is wise in warfare, trustworthy and brave, valuable both to his leaders and other men around him.

You need to see yourself this way; you have entered what might be a long, hard campaign that could last for years. As you endure and choose to do what's right, will you become a mighty man of God. You will be both pleasing to the Lord and a man who can have a tremendous spiritual influence on others as you show what God can do in a man even though he is not in a pleasant relationship. In time, God will use you to help others in the same situation as you are presently in now, using you to strengthen, counsel and encourage others to hang in there and do God's will. After all, God's way is always the best way. Not only will this strategy help you in your marriage, it will influence your perspective at work, around friends, extended family, and in church. I know it is God's will for you and your wife to have a good marriage. That is His intent. But because of Sin, Satan and the world's strong influence, many marriages are secretly caught in this kind of miserable relationship like Mikes.

If you're reading this book because you're one of those men who are living this kind of life, read on! But beware, it will ask you to take bold steps as a Christian to follow God's will.

CHAPTER ONE

Finding Out Who You Really Are

Personal Holiness

I have found that when a Christian man is in a situation with a difficult wife, he can easily give in to various sins like anger, frustration, outbursts of verbal abuse, lusting after other women, and even immorality. In order to please God you must first realize you are a soldier in a spiritual battle. Maybe at this point you are a tired soldier, even a deserter, but you are one who needs to change. You might be thinking at this point, *"Me? My mean wife is the one that needs to change!"* But who's reading this book? You are! But that's good. Most wives at this point in their marriage see themselves as a victim of both bad circumstances and a lousy husband. At least you are willing now in your life to take a hard and honest look at yourself and change, not ultimately for your wife, but for the glory of God and what He wants to do in your life. And if you are really serious about this, you will find true direction, hope and peace in your life even amongst turmoil. The bible says *"There was peace at the cross."* How was that possible? Their was turmoil, pain, death, cursing and hatred toward Christ. There was peace there because

11

Jesus was doing fully the will of God. The same is true with you. Maybe not now, but the goal of this book is to get you to that point. What Point you may ask? Of walking maturely by the Spirit in obedience to God's word. This change comes by being very honest with yourself, your situation, and your sin. You can make a very good list of all the bad things your wife is doing to you. But the issue at this point is not your wife. She does have her sinful issues and repentance is hoped for, but she has not chosen repentance, so you must look at your own heart, motives and intents and measure them against God's Word. Then you must intently choose to change, no matter the personal cost, giving up dreams and desires, all to win the war, all to please Christ. Many men I have counseled choose to stay passive and unresolved in this difficult situation, simply because they may lose a house, money, cars or their reputations.

One thing not discussed to often anymore is the concept that as a Christian you have died to selfish desires; you're dead to these things! And you have been resurrected to life as a slave to serve who? Christ and His ways. Your goal in life is to serve Him first and above all else to please him in all you do and say. Your problems are usually associated with the deeds of the flesh and self.

Therefore we were buried with Him through baptism into death, that just as Christ was raised from the dead by the glory of the Father, even so we also should walk in newness of life...Know this, that our old man was crucified with Him, that the body of sin might be done away with, that we should no longer be slaves of sin...Likewise you also, reckon yourselves to be dead indeed to sin, but alive to God in Christ Jesus our Lord. Therefore do not let sin reign in your mortal body, that you should obey its lusts **(Rom 6:4, 6, 11-13).**

That means in your marriage, you are to remain humble, merciful, loving your rebellious wife as Christ loves the church. And most of all, you must see your wife as someone in need of ministry, long term perhaps. It's easy to love those who love back; it's hard to love those who despise you. But Jesus said love even your enemies.

But I say to you who hear: Love your enemies, do good to those who hate you, bless those who curse you and pray for those who spitefully use you **(Luke 6:27-28).**

This statement by Jesus is radical. It goes against everything the world says to do in situations like these. But if you are a Christian, radical change is the norm not the exception.

Your wife may actually see you as an enemy. But as you endure, humble yourself and love her as Christ loves you, even when you disobey Him and sin. Instead, choose to walk as Jesus' walked and you will grow in your faith and obedience to Christ. You see, if you're dead to self, you really shouldn't care if your wife puts you down verbally or says evil against you, you're dead to self. To be Christ- like means you will suffer!

For this is the will of God, that by doing good you may put to silence the ignorance of foolish men...For this is commendable, if because of conscience towards God one endures grief, suffering wrongfully. For what credit is it if, when you are beaten for your faults, you take it patiently?

But when you do good and suffer, if you take it patiently, this is commendable before God. For to this you were called because Christ also suffered for us, leaving us an example, that you should follow His steps (**1 Pet 2:15, 19-21**).

The Savior has raised you to serve Him, not self. He was left alone on the cross to die for those who loved Him not. He still loved them through His actions on that cross. So must be your intent in life. Since you are dead to self and selfish desires, don't let pride offend others or defend self. I'm going to say something that goes directly against what the world teaches. *Strive in your life to rid yourself of personal, prideful identity and instead set forth Christ-likeness, His attitude, and seek first His kingdom and will.*

But seek first the Kingdom of God and His righteousness, and all these things will be added to you (**Matt 6:33**).

Dead people have no identity. This is what really separates religiously minded people from those who have chosen to follow Christ. Those who are true Christians have realized their depraved condition before God as sinners, those who fully deserve God's wrath. But they have accepted God's free gift of grace through Christ's sacrifice on the cross.

True followers of Christ have definite characteristics that prove they are genuine believers.

1. They are *obedient* to Christ and His Word, no matter how they feel or the repercussions involved. *"If you love Me, keep My commandments" (John 14:15).*

2. Because they are obedient to His Word, they remain faithful to Him

    If you abide in Me, and My words abide in you...My Father is glorified by this, that you bear much fruit, and so prove to be my disciples (John 15:7-8).

3. A true follower *perseveres* daily in obedience to His Word. This is the fruit or evidence of real faith. The word "abide" in 15:8 means to habitually abide in His Word.

4. A true follower exhibits a *supernatural love* that surpasses the world's kind of love. He will love even his enemies. *"A new commandment I give you, that you love one another; as I have loved you, that you also love one another. By this all will know that you are my disciples, if you have love for one another" (John 13:35).*

5   True followers are people who *consistently put others before themselves.* They are truly humble. *"It is enough for a disciple that he be like his teacher, and a servant like his master" (Matt 10:25).*

6. A true follower *puts Christ first in everything.* The hatred mentioned in the verse below is a lesser love. Jesus is calling His followers to a sincere devotion. They are to cultivate a love for Him that supersedes everything else in this world, even their own life, *"If anyone comes to Me and does not hate his father and mother, wife and children, brothers and sisters, yes even his own life also, he cannot be My disciple...So likewise, whoever of you does not forsake all that he has cannot be My disciple" (Luke 14:26, 33).* The

hatred here is actually not an angered hatred, but a lesser love. Jesus is calling His followers to such a devotion to Him and His purposes that their attachments to everything else in this world appears as hatred (See also Luke 16:13; Matt 10:37).

7. A true follower of Christ *denies himself.*

If anyone desires to come after Me, let him deny himself, and take up his cross, and follow Me. For whoever desires to save his life will lose it, but whoever loses his life for my sake will find it. For what profit is it to a man if he gains the whole world, and loses his own soul? Or what will a man give in exchange for his human spirit (Matt 16:24-26).

As a Christian, denying self is our ongoing battle of desires, possessions and dreams. Many arguments with wives are started over selfish desires concerning money, ideas or other possessions. When a man comes to the point of giving it all up to God, showing ownership of nothing in this world, he will find peace and true contentment, even when his wife tries to be greedy or selfish. There will be this graciousness that overcomes one as he yields all to Him and really proves he believes in the sovereignty and power of God to take care of Him.

As a true believer, we have all died to selfish desires (Romans 6). The problem is we haven't died to all our self deeds-the habitually difficult sinful things that cause so many problems. This is the reason men in difficult marriage situations have struggles. It's like having one foot in the grave and one in the world: pride, greed over money and ownership of material possessions- all these things cloud one's vision of the true purpose we have been called to. Pastors are not the only ones who are in full time ministry. Yes, they might make their living at it, but every man, in full time ministry or as a regular guy working in the world is called to full time discipleship. All Christians are to follow Christ and live out daily His attributes and will. Not just on Sundays. True peace and contentment comes only when we give up the desire to have total control of money, material possessions, and the need to "feel loved." True freedom comes as one truly dies to selfish deeds and strives to be Christ-like in love and actions, putting Him first in all things. This doesn't mean men act irresponsibly as fathers, husbands, the paying of bills, the handling of money, or their job. God expects them to be good stewards of all the things He has given them. But many a heart pain and internal struggle occurs because the man doesn't like the way the wife handles money, time or material possessions, or the lack of care she has about the health of their marriage.

Often men imagine how it would be to escape from their situation or what it would mean to have true and lasting peace and contentment. The problem is that even as Christians, we may think true happiness is found in a good marriage, plenty of money in the bank account, plenty of material possessions, a good job, or even sex. Thinking this way leads to false expectations and can fool even the most experienced believer. Problems usually are born when you let emotions and imaginations supersede your knowledge of God's principles for how to respond Biblically in those situations. You will find lasting peace and contentment, even in the midst of turmoil and a lack of a good marriage, by growing toward Christ-likeness in obedience to God's Word and principle, practicing those principles in all your daily life situations and realizing that God is in control.

Sure it's God's will that your marriage be good and right, fulfilling for both you and your wife. But for many of you this is not the case and you don't have to walk each day as though a dark cloud hung over you with no hope but only despair. You may have a false idea in your heart of hearts that if you could get out of this marriage, your life would once again be happy and full of peace. The truth is it won't! As said earlier, true peace is walking in the battle as a wise and faithful soldier, following the commanders orders no matter the situation or his own personal feelings. In the midst of this battle the wise man, no matter how immature or lowly they may think themselves, must choose to strive for holiness. Striving to learn how Christ would want them to act in every situation in their lives according to the principles laid down already for us in Scripture. This means that the man in this situation needs to focus much time on prayer and Bible study to see how God thinks and what principles He has laid down to deal with holiness and growing up over the years to being a man of God. Many times husbands focus so much on their wives and all the daily problems they are having, that they lose their real focus on Christ and growing to be like Him in all their *thinking, actions, and their treatment of others.* From all my years as a Christian, I have found that if a man has a right focus he will deal much better with the daily responsibilities and struggles of life. He will show more compassion, more agape love, more wise thinking, and a better Christ-like attitude in all situations, even the difficult ones. He will be a good soldier in the midst of battle, doing what is right. The next section deals with some things I have found that lead men down a path of wrong decision- making and actions, which must be repented of later. These concern the very important matter of feelings. Over the last several years, I have worked with men who found themselves in these hard situations, and almost in every case they are living daily by their feelings, dealing with anger, pride, selfishness and the lack of love, causing more destruction for themselves, their wives and their children.

Learning to be obedient to God's word, not your feelings

Allowing feelings to rule your decision-making process is a huge problem among Christian married men. I don't think there has been one counseling situation over the years where this was not a part of the problem. Almost every man I have ever counseled, in these difficult marriage situations has been living a feeling orientated kind of lifestyle. Their sinful actions result from feelings which cause harmful repercussions for many people they know, even their children. God gave us feelings and emotions for a very good reason. The problem comes when we let them run our lives, making foolish decisions based upon the feelings of the moment. A man who is feeling-oriented will live a life like a roller coaster; ups and downs will become a lifestyle. Eventually people like this become very emotionally disturbed and are usually labeled, at the extremes, "bi-polar" by the medical and psychological professions. In reality, for the Christian man, a bi-polar person is no more than one who has been trained to live by their emotions, making decisions and letting their twisted minds be shoved back and forth according to how they feel. No discernment, no wise principles to the making of decisions based upon God's Word, just floating along making one wrong decision after another, causing more and more harm to themselves and others. Slowly they build thought patterns that create more wrong decisions, like building blocks of destruction.

This kind of feeling-oriented lifestyle is one of the main reasons so many men have outbursts of anger, are greedy, have a lot of hate, and lust problems. They have trained themselves incorrectly in their thinking. By the time they come to me for counseling they feel trapped, as if there is no hope. The key to true Biblical change in a man's life is to realize the harm of the feeling-oriented lifestyle. He needs to become a man who is commandment-oriented, being stead-fastly obedient to God's Word no matter how he feels. When his wife is being difficult, saying things that are full of bitterness, anger and failing even to have any common sense, he can be calm and at peace with himself and God. Even during these heated times he can maintain his composure, speaking and thinking words of wisdom, love and compassion.

You might be saying to yourself, *"not me, I could never do that"*. But God says you can! In fact He commands you to be that way: ***"No temptation has overtaken you except such as is common to man; but God is faithful, who will not allow you to be tempted beyond what you are able, but with the temptations will also make the way of escape, that you may be able to bear it", (I Cor. 10:13); "the Lord knows how to deliver the godly out of temptations" (2 Peter 2:9).*** God will never tell you to do something you can't do. The problem is not with God, it's with you and your own desires. Maybe deep down inside you don't strive for holiness because either you want your wife to eventually leave so you can think you're "free," or maybe you just want people to feel sorry for you. All of these things are lies that can be easily-accepted, making you feel good. If you ever choose these things and leave your wife, all you will be doing is simply taking your entire bad personal luggage into your next relationship. You will also inherit another woman's bad luggage and together you will learn to hate each other even more than you hated your previous spouse. This is the reason the percentage of divorces are doubled in second marriages from the first ones. When Mike came in for counseling this is where he was. At times he was full of anger and disgust at his wife. But the real problem with Mike was his life long decision to live by his feelings. Things like greed over the misuse of money, mean words spoken to him and a lack of love from his wife caused him to be miserable, out of control of his situations and eventually leaving him hopeless. I knew what the problem was with Mike. But was Mike willing to take the bold challenge to take a hard look at himself and change to please God? That's the crux in most counseling situations like Mikes. Sadly to say most choose to live in sin and eventually divorce. But there is always a small remnant of men who truly show they are Christians and desire to follow Christ, no matter the cost. Let me give you an illustration I use in counseling that helps people picture in their minds what I've been saying. It's called the 'kite illustration'.

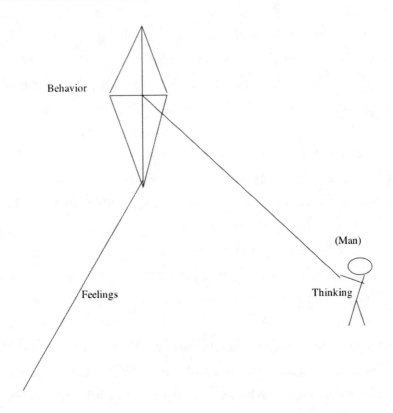

The kite illustration represents our lives and the decision-making processes, all of which can cause us to fall into many destructive sinful traps if we do not live Biblically. This is the very reason people are in for counseling. The man represents the thinking process. The kite itself represents behavior, which is greatly affected by the man's thinking. He may turn the kite anyway he wishes. The tail of the kite, which moves according to where the kite itself goes, represents our feelings.

Let's take the example of Steve, one of my counselee's. He was a bright young man who initially did very well in the business world. Steve would make a wise decision that would affect his behavior (kite), after which his feelings/emotions would follow.

That's the way it's supposed to work. Your thinking affects your behavior (how you act), and your feelings will follow suit, right? Sadly, Steve decided to live by his feelings. He reversed the whole Biblical process. He let his feelings (the kite's tail) make choices for him. How he felt that day, whether he was upset, angry, depressed, all affected his behavior, which in turn affected his thinking. After many years of doing this, Steve's career went down the tubes, along with his marriage. Because he was feeling-oriented, he acted and made decisions on how he felt that minute, hour or day. Steve was living a roller coaster kind of lifestyle. He was lacking in steadfastness, integrity, honesty, and morality. Even though he claimed to believe in God and attended church once in a while, he lacked true discipleship with other men and a desire to please God in all he does. When depressed he would see the world as bleak, thus his decisions reflected that. When he felt no hope he would sink into immorality, drinking, or anything else that met his "felt need". If work was tough, when Steve got home he was usually in a rotten mood toward his wife and children, even though they did nothing to deserve his sinful behavior. In time, his world came crashing down on him. Through Biblical counseling he was able to overcome these sinful patterns, turn things around and start making wise choices, no matter how he felt. As he strove to please Christ in all his ways, Steve grew spiritually and became a man of integrity, honesty, and was used of God to help others. But this did not happen overnight. It took Steve years of learning and practicing Biblical principles. You can do the same thing in your life. *In fact, your difficult wife can be a blessing to you. It will be in your own home that you can put into practice what God wants you to do.* This sentence may seem strange, but your wife can be a means used by God to actually help grow you spiritually. It is through affliction that we can often grow the most.

CHAPTER TWO

Home: The Proving Ground For The Spirit's Work

O ne of the other key elements in getting through your diffi-cult situation is being proactive in the home. *Be proactive not inactive or reactive.* Mike had come to the point in his marriage that he tried everything to stay late at work so he wouldn't be around his wife. But when at home, he worked long hours in his garage or out in the yard for the same reason. When he did talk to his wife, it was usually with short, impatient words and at times just sharp, rude remarks toward her. After coming to counseling Mike learned to do the opposite with his wife, to actually being proactive with her. Listening, learning and reacting in a Godly way. This wasn't easy at first for Mike because he had so trained himself to do the oppo-site with his wife and always having the feeling he had to be on the offensive with her. Over time and out of his love for God, he started practicing these things in his life, all to her amazement. This is what the Apostle Peter was teaching in 1 Peter 3:7 on how husbands are to study their wives in order to better minister to them.

This is the practical side of what will follow, communicating with your wife, talking and listening to her. But concerning this topic, here is what our friend Mike would do on many occasions. After a hard day's work he would go home, expecting his wife to have a dinner ready. Then he would hope to plop down on the couch and watch TV, another way of avoidance.

Some men may not watch TV, but they do other things to keep themselves busy, such as the internet, sports or hobbies. You get the point. Mike's wife also worked. She had started her own business and it was doing well. They had no children at this point in their marriage. She would come home; make dinner, vacuum the house and clean, wash clothes, then at some time during the night take care of business paperwork, all the while Mike would lie around doing his own thing and wondering why she was so "sinfully cranky". I'm not saying her sinful behavior was justified; she needed to repent and do things God's way also. But the whole situation would be frustrating wouldn't it?

So how could Mike turn things around and be proactive instead of inactive and reactive all the time? To start with, turn off the TV, Internet, sports, hobbies, and think of ways to help out around the house. Close the shades, take out the trash, cook dinner, clean the house, work with your wife, talk to her, listen to her, think through what she shares with you, even if it's not about your marriage. As a start, this is what I counseled mike to do. It was part of being proactive. He didn't wait to be told what to do around the house, he found things to do. He also found things to do *for* his wife, like giving her flowers or bringing home small gifts after work, or even leaving thank-you notes. They were small but sincere things. Now I must admit that at first things didn't go so smoothly for Mike. Her "meanness" did not go away overnight. But Mike was doing the right thing; he was loving his wife as Christ loved the church, sacrificially.

He was living above his situation, which God calls men to do. At first Mike and his wife had no deep discussions about their troubled marriage. For some time they just talked about the day, her sore feet, money issues and engaged in other small talk. But now he was focused on her. He actually showed an interest in her and what she was saying, and without saying so, she saw a difference in him. He was consistent, compassionate, loving, and caring. He was acting Christ-like.

I want to reemphasize something here that is very important, *consistent proactiveness is the key to impactfulness.* Don't do this for a week and go back to your old ways, thinking all is fixed. Be consistent, even if she doesn't respond positively to this change in your life; be consistent for a higher reason, to please God. Being proactive means you're not going to be

> A man must live above his situation. This brings growth and influences to others

reactive. Before this time, you had to react to all her critical words because it bothered you that she would talk while you watched your favorite TV show; and it was always during the best part of the show, the climax. Such behavior is merely reactive. Being proactive means you plan ahead of an event, thinking it through, using your time and talents to the betterment.

This is what you do at home. Before arriving, realize that your time is not your own, its God's time. And God wants you to be proactive in ministering to your wife. Believe me, after several weeks of her seeing your consistency in helping around the house and your willingness to listen; there is usually a change in attitude on her part. But you may ask, "What if there is no change? What if she is still very difficult? What do I do then?" Some may say give up and go back to the TV, the old standby. For heavens sake, no! And I mean that literally. God wants you to be a godly man with integrity, one who strives to live out Biblical principles, no matter if the situation is bad or good. Circumstances do not dictate your attitude or lifestyle, like so many Christians think they do. Actually greater strength is shown when a man can keep his cool and patience amidst turmoil. Instead, the man of God is to remain steadfast in doing what's right. Be consistent at being proactive in doing what God would have you to do.

Learning the Art of Listening and Talking

Once the TV is off and you're being proactive, practice the art of listening to your wife. God gave you two ears and one mouth, which should teach you that you should be listening twice as much as speaking. Listen to her carefully, learn to discern and understand her thoughts, and seek to study her so you can eventually respond in a mature and sensible way. Even the little chats should be moments of interest.

Husbands likewise, dwell with your wife with understanding [study her] giving honor to the wife, as to the weaker vessel, and as being heirs together of the grace of life, that your prayers may not be hindered (**I Pet 3:7**).

You are commanded to submit to a loving duty of being sensitive to the needs, fears, and feelings of your wife. You must subordinate your needs to hers, whether she is a Christian or not.

> **Husbands, love your wives and do not be bitter towards them (Col 3:19).**

You are here commanded to love your wife, even when she has treated you wrongly. This kind of love is the highest form of love God Himself has bestowed upon you. It is the same kind of love God shows you when you rebel against Him. This verse also says that you are not to be bitter. The Greek actually says, *"Stop being bitter"* or *"Do not have the habit of being bitter."* This presupposes that the wife is doing something that would normally cause a husband to become bitter. But for you, being a follower of Christ, you are commanded not to take this route. So if you are to put off bitterness, what do you practice instead? God's love, forgiveness, and patience.

Communication is also a way of loving your wife as Christ loves the church. When you communicate with your wife, it takes self-control, discipline, spiritual discernment, focus and a controlled tongue. It means mastering your feelings and not letting them control you. Many times your speech creates very large divisions in the home.

> **For we stumble in many ways. If anyone does not stumble in what he says, he is a mature man, able to control the body as well (James 3:2).**

Taking control of your speech is a great virtue with God, and it can be a way of bringing Him glory through your life. But if you are not on guard with your speech it can grieve the Holy Spirit and cause further harm to others, like your wife and children. Your present speech will reveal the real you, especially in the home. What comes out of your mouth reveals your heart. Real examination on your part is needed concerning your speech. God the Spirit already knows; why not be honest with yourself too? Everything Christ communicated was holy, clear, purposeful, and delivered at the right time, using discernment. There are six things you should deeply consider here concerning your speech. Read them carefully and look up the Scriptures that relate to each.

1. A husband must want to please God more than anything else in this life. Christ must be the foremost. He must desire to please God above anyone else, including himself (2 Cor 5:9).

2. A husband must desire to lead a humble life toward God and others. A humble communicator is a wise communicator. He puts the other person's needs above his own (Eph 4:1-3).

3. A husband must understand that everything he says will be accountable before God; that means every word you speak to your wife. Christ, God the Spirit, and the Father hear every word you say (Matt 12:36).

4. A husband must learn how to listen more than talk. In the middle of a disagreement, listening sometimes takes the backstage. But if you want to grow spiritually, learn the art of holding yourself back. Learn to listen and see your wife's point of view, seeking to see things her way (James 1:19; Prov 18:13).

5. A husband must know that good communication is not just words, it is tone of voice, eye contact, body language and

deeds, facial expressions, rolling of eyes, and anything that could expose your evil heart (James 4:17).

6. A husband must come to the point where he realizes that good communication takes time. Even when you don't want to, seek to sit down and talk to your wife, even over the little things (Rom 12:10-12).

Breaking the False expectation that Life Should Be Free of Hardship

Most of his life Steve had a certain picture of what marriage should look like. It was much like the old TV show "leave it to Beaver." He was shocked to see the wife he loved and desired to marry, years later becoming one he hated and wished would go away.

Most people falsely think life should be without struggles, conflicts, or little problems, especially for Christians. That's why many Christian husbands are dismayed and fall into depression. They think hardships should happen to others but not to them. Having this kind of false image can lead a man to judge all afflictions and trouble as bad and something to be avoided at all costs. At times you may feel like the unluckiest person alive to have married the wrong woman, whose second car is a broom.

But this false, worldly picture must be reshaped and replaced with the true Biblical picture. Life is at times hard. Conflict and problems are inevitable, emotional pain is a reality, and sometimes bad things happen; yes, even to you as a Christian. Today's false teaching says that if you are truly holy, life will always be full of happiness, bliss, health and wealth, and without any trouble. But reality teaches us differently, even for Christians! Most of the men of God in the Bible

31

suffered even though they were holy, loved God, and followed Him. Even the Son of God, as innocent as He was, suffered at the hands of evil people most of His ministry. *The key is understanding that the measure of your godliness isn't your circumstances but instead how you respond to them, either with sinful thinking and behavior or with Biblical integrity and principles.* Biblical convictions are built over time and practice. As you study God's Word and integrate it's principles into everyday life situations, spiritual growth will occur. Then you will be able to withstand any circumstance that comes your way, even that of living with a difficult wife.

Believe it or not God has actually ordained all that's happening in your life to help you grow in your sanctification.

Winning the Battle in Your Mind and Imagination

Remember our friend Mike? Well, one of the things that would really upset and eventually ruin Mike's whole day was his habit of going over past arguments in his mind. While driving and at work he would spend hours in his imagination going over and over those events. He would go over his wife's mean words of spite and revenge. He would then go over his words. The battle in the mind would rage for hours while his emotions got all worked up. It affected his work, his emotions and attitudes, and especially his spiritual walk. Instead of mediating on God's Word, prayer, and learning to be thankful, his mind was reenacting verbal World War with his wife. It was as if the whole world was blocked out by the scene in his home of his wife and him; finally he mentally reenacted the picture so much that his wife became a demon-possessed person and he an innocent lamb. These events would happen so much every day that it almost drove Mike crazy. His work became hampered. His spiritual walk seemed empty. Hope and despair filled his life, and his attitude was so rotten that he felt like running away from it all. Have you ever been in this situation?

The answer is probably, yes! In fact, you're probably wondering if I'm writing about you. Mike was so engrossed in this sinful habit that he began talking to himself. The guys at work would often see him doing this and felt bad for him, thinking, *"Poor mike, and such a nice guy to lose his mind like that."* This scenario is the natural fruit of so much "self-talk." Self-talk is becoming so engrossed in your imagination about your difficult situation that the scene in your mind becomes real to your lips. Many times Mike had no idea he was doing this. After hours of dwelling on his wife's words and the situation, anger would build until by the time he was off work, his attitude was totally sinful. When he arrived home, the verbal warfare would start all over again as if there was no time lapse.

Can you imagine after days and weeks of doing this, training his mind to act that way, why Mike had problems? In reality, Mike was his biggest enemy. His choice to dwell on those events caused most of his problems and much sinful fruit came from those actions.

Mike's problem is actually extremely common. God gave us the capacity for memory. It's a wonderful gift. The problem is that our sinful natures use it in ways that lead us into more destructive, sinful patterns. So how can Mike be helped? More than likely you've been in Mike's situation many times.

Finding the ultimate answer

The answer is simple yet hard to enact because of a sinful habit you have been doing for a long time. You have been training yourself for years to mentally reenact events of profound hurt and pain so that it has become a habit. It takes very little effort to start this pattern of thinking. Within seconds you're back in the battle scene. But I can say with certainty that God has given you an answer. The answer is a lot like a coin; it has two distinct sides but is one. This "coin" is your relationship with Christ. You have been joined eternally to Christ at your regeneration/new birth. This relationship cannot be shaken, not because of your worth or self righteousness, but because of God's grace and election of you, all too eventually bring glory to His name. The two sides, though, are important for you to understand. On the one side is God's work on your behalf. He elected you before time began (Eph 1:4). He regenerated you, giving you salvation through your repentance and faith in Christ to be your Savior (Acts 5:14; 1 Tim 4:12). You were supposed to die to your selfish ways and be spiritually resurrected to live for Christ everyday (Rom 4:25; 8:34; 1 Cor 15:18-19; 14-17). You were given the Spirit of God to dwell in you forever (Rom 8:11), giving you the ability/power to overcome sin and act righteously. You were given the Holy Scriptures to guide you in this life to become Christ-like (Psa 119:11 97; 113; 167; Col 3:16). With all of this accomplished comes the other side of the coin, your choice. This is where the break down always occurs. Never with God but with you. This is because you choose to sin. Instead of doing things God's way, you choose to do things your way, with your sinful nature guiding you, tossing God aside and choose the sinful, inferior path, which causes failure, destruction, and hurt for yourself, your wife and above all, you are grieving the Spirit Himself.

So what are you suppose to do to stop this tragic pattern and move on to the right path? Let's take a look at the Scriptures and see God's way.

Taking Every Thought Captive

1. You must intently take control of your mind and begin thinking as Christ would have you think. This won't be easy because you have trained yourself over the years to easily drift into sinful patterns. You must be on your guard. You must actively bring all your thoughts captive to the obedience of Christ. There is really no excuse not to. God the Spirit has given you the ability to do this very thing.

   For the weapons of our warfare are not carnal but mighty in God for pulling down strongholds, casting down arguments and every high thing that exalts itself against the knowledge of God, bring every thought into captivity to the obedience of Christ, and being ready to punish all disobedience when your obedience is fulfilled (2 Cor 10:4-6).

2. Your thoughts are not only to be captured and brought under submission; they are to be critiqued by God's Word. We live in a world of so many false beliefs, even within the church, people lack discernment to know what is true and what is of this satanic system. Remember that Satan is an intelligent being who has been around for thousands of years. He has tricked great men, kings, and authorities by the thousands. He is an intelligent being who is quite experienced. He has sown his crafty wisdom in such a way today that even believers have swallowed hook, line, and sinker many of His lies. Things like blame-shifting, deceit, white lies, lustful immorality, prideful self-worth and self-esteem, and

many more are not of God. Yet God's valuable life changing principles aren't taken seriously by believers today; however God takes them very seriously. This is why every believer needs to become a good theologian. That doesn't mean you have to get a degree, but what it does mean is that God has given you the capability to read, study, and understand Scripture. The truth of this gives you the ability to discern between truth and error.

For the Word of God is living and powerful, and sharper than any two-edged sword, piercing even to the division of soul and spirit, and of joints and marrow, and is a discerner of the thoughts and intents of the heart **(Heb 4:12).**

3. There needs to be transparency in your life before God so your conscience can be made clear and your mind at ease as you honestly face yourself and all your ways. In addition, you must chose to intently do things God's way instead of yours. You should be actively searching your motives on why you do or say certain things. Why did you say or do those things to your wife? What are the real reasons? When you choose to sin, it is because you either considered something of more value than your relationship to God, or you just selfishly wanted something, like sex, money, love, respect, or some possession. David went through this. He had power, riches, and women. Yet in all this he found no peace, contentment, or a clear conscience before God; not

until he came to repentance and followed God's ways. At that point in his life David could say,

Search me, O God, and know my heart [motives], try me and know my anxieties; and see if there is any wicked way in me, and lead me in he way everlasting **(Psa 139:23-24).**

Let God in on your thought life, your plans, and your motives. He will use His inspired Word to correct you and give you a clear and honest perspective on the real issues. You will begin to see your wife in a different light. And in all this I can promise you something else. You will have a peace that will never be understood by the world.

Be anxious for nothing, but in everything by prayer and supplication, with thanksgiving, let your requests be known to God; and the peace of God which surpasses all understanding will guard your hearts and minds through Christ Jesus **(Phil 4:6-7).**

Making a Change that Lasts in Your Life
The Biblical Answer to Help Change You

You might not have realized this, but Biblical change should be a part of your life until you breathe your last; it is not just for the young. Change should always be your personal goal, but it is sometimes hard.

I spoke to you in your prosperity, but you said, 'I will not hear'. This has been your manner from your youth. That you did not obey my voice (**Jer 22:21**).

Over the years I have found two basic reasons why people don't change. First, they are unwilling because their sin is either more important to them functionally than God, acting in rebellion. Or secondly, they may not know how to change. They feel stuck in a trap with no way out. You cannot change the past, but you can change your present situation. If you choose to dwell on the past and live presently with all that bitterness, change will not occur. The past is gone, so it can't be changed; what needs to be changed is you. The past can only be dealt with in the present by forgiveness, reconciliation, and repentance. Repentance, a changing of directions, is a change of mind and motives that leads to a change in lifestyle (see Acts 20:26). Your goal as a Christian is to please and glorify God, to press on daily with the following goal in mind:

Brethren, I do not count myself to have apprehended, but one thing I do, forgetting those things which are behind and reaching forward to those things which are ahead, I press toward the goal for the prize of the upward call of God in Christ Jesus (**Phil 3:13-14**).

Do you want changes that last? It is this book's goal to direct toward change, but ultimately that change must come from your heart and the Spirit's work. People develop habits of sinful thinking and lifestyles. But deep down inside, out of a love for God, there must be a desire for dehabituation and rehabituation, or to put it a simpler way, a need to put-off sin and put-on righteous ways (Eph. 4).

Your manner of life is a habitual way of life. God gave you a gift called habit. Because of the fall, though, you can easily and naturally choose sinful ways that can, over time, develop into bad life pattern of habits.

For everyone who partakes of milk is unskilled in the word of righteousness, for he is a babe. But solid food belongs to those who are of full age, that is, those who by reason of practice have their senses exercised to discern both good and evil **(Heb 5:13ff)**.

You need to be taught that if you practice what God tells you, living obediently to His Word and principles, it will become a part of your life. In actuality, choosing to follow God's principles brings discipline into your life.

The diagram below illustrates how habits are put off and put on for Christians, all through the power of the Spirit in obedience to the Word. Sinful habits are put-off daily by intently saying no to them, no matter how you feel, and instead intently putting on and applying the Biblical way in every situation.

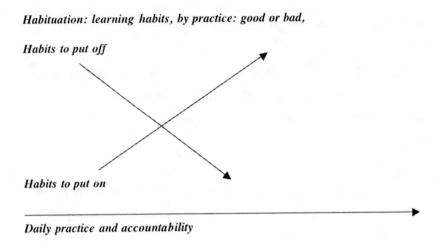

Habituation: learning habits, by practice: good or bad,

Habits to put off

Habits to put on

Daily practice and accountability

YOUR PERSONAL HABITUATION LISTS

Take a few moments and fill in the blanks below. Write out what things in your life you should put-off, and then on the other side write out the things you are to put-on in there place.

Put-off List   Put-on List

_____   _____

_____   _____

_____   _____

_____   _____

*Therefore **putting away** lying, let each one of you **speak the truth**...Let him **who stole** steal no longer, but rather **let him labor, working** with his hands what is good...Let **no corrupt word** proceed*

*out of your mouth, but what is good for necessary **edification**, that it may impart grace to the hearers...let all bitterness, wrath, anger, clamor and evil speaking be put away from you, with all malice. And be kind to one another, tenderhearted, forgiving one another, even as God in Christ forgave you* (Eph 4:25-32).

*But now you yourselves are **to put off** all these: anger, wrath, malice, blasphemy, filthy language out of your mouth. Do not lie to one another, since you have **put off** the old man with his deeds and have put on the new man who is renewed in knowledge according to the image of Him who created him...Therefore as the elect of God, holy and beloved, **put on** tender mercies, kindness, humility, meekness, longsuffering, bearing with one another, and forgiving one another; even as Christ forgave you, so you must also. But above all things, **put on** love, which is the bond of maturity* (Col 3:8-14).

In the above verses, we see the put-off/put-on principle of Scripture. As fallen creatures saved by the pure grace of God, we are to put off the old ways and put on and practice the Christ-like ways in every area of life. Through the power of the Spirit and obedience to the Word of God, you are to ***change***.

SEVEN ELEMENTS FOR CHANGE

Maybe without your realizing it, there are stages of change that every human goes through, whether a believer or not. We all change one way or the other. In not choosing to intently go God's way, people will naturally change from good to worse because of their fallen nature. All are prone to bend that way. It takes little effort to sin. Just watch your own children. You didn't have to teach them to be selfish, greedy and hateful as babies. Where did this come from? Their little fallen; sinful natures. But for the believer it takes intention of heart to choose to follow God's principles and ways in his daily life, in every situation, good or hard. In my many years as a Christian and in all my counseling, I've noticed the stages a believer will go through in changing to do things God's way.

1. Becoming aware of the sinful practice that must be put off. You must look into your own life, honestly see what sinful things you are doing and what good things you are not doing, and discover how Christ wants you to change.

2. Finding the Biblical alternative. You must find out from Scripture what Christ wants you to replace for the thing you put off.

3. Restructuring life for change. What places, events or situations in your life need to change to help you conform to Christ's way.

4. Breaking away from impediments that influence sin. What influences do you have in your life that tempts you to sin?

5. Being accountable to others for change-God has no lone rangers. Find someone in your church you can have as a discipler who will hold you accountable for change. Open up and be transparent with them.

6. Stressing spiritual growth. This should be your ultimate goal everyday, striving to bring God glory.

7. Daily practicing Biblical habits, being responsible, being consistent.

As you start your life toward change, there should be the recognition of something very important, something that I have found over the years in counseling that a lot of Christian men do, sometimes that happens without realizing the deadly consequences. People live their lives in categories. They tend to have a religious one and then a worldly one. The two are many times separated, with a little mingling at times, especially during crisis events. During these times, people want God to enter the worldly events until the emergency has past; then the walls of separation go up again. On Sunday they are religious, come Monday they are back to their old sinful self. Anger, greed, selfishness, gossip and pride all return as the person gets through the week.

The problem with this kind of living is it's totally unbiblical, something the Holy Spirit within you strives against. It is also very destructive to any spiritual growth. Many a man I have known who has lived this kind of lifestyle has experienced all kinds of internal conflicts, struggles, and emotional pain. The major problem with this kind of living is that the Holy Spirit wants the whole you. He wants every area of your life impacted by the inspired Word of God everyday. Living a categorical life causes a lack of consistent, ongoing growth toward Christ-likeness in your speech, thinking, and actions. Instead, what you end up being is just another religious hypocrite.

HOW RIGHTEOUSNESS SHOULD AFFECT ALL AREAS OF YOUR LIFE

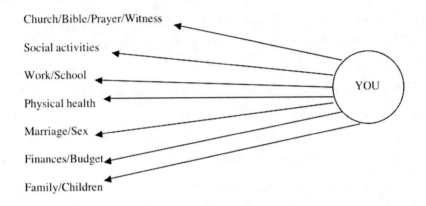

Church/Bible/Prayer/Witness

Social activities

Work/School

Physical health

Marriage/Sex

Finances/Budget

Family/Children

YOU

Many times the Christian easily slips into apathy, sinful habits, and a lethargic attitude that seems to permeate almost every area of his life. Reading the Bible, worshiping God, desiring to grow in Christ-likeness lessens. For anyone, this is a dangerous place to be, because you're now open to the destructive powers of sin and Satan. During seasons like this, a lot of damage can be done to greatly harm you, your family, and the church. But how does it all start? The illustration below shows you. It starts small and then grows to be a very large sin issue.

HOW IT STARTS

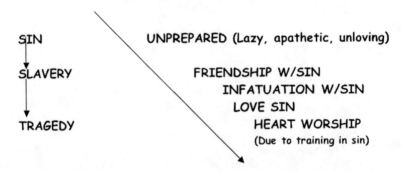

SIN

SLAVERY

TRAGEDY

UNPREPARED (Lazy, apathetic, unloving)

FRIENDSHIP W/SIN
INFATUATION W/SIN
LOVE SIN
HEART WORSHIP
(Due to training in sin)

It all starts with small steps of spiritual casualness or indifference and a lack of sensitivity to right and wrong. It all begins with small steps of disobedience. Many times simple idols of the heart.

"Do not merely listen to the word and so deceive yourself; do what it says" (**James 1:22**).

"The Lord said, "Be careful, or you will be enticed to turn away and worship other gods" (**Deut. 11:16**).

Choosing sin

1. You become very comfortable with this sin because of practice
2. You now do it automatically in any situation
3. You do this sin without much conscience thought or decision

Destruction

HOW TO HELP PEOPLE CHANGE

It is interesting to note that both psychology and Biblical counselors can agree on one thing-*that people need to change.* The differences come as to the method of that change and the end result of it. Psychologists and integrationist counselors can't agree on these things. There are about three hundred schemes of counseling presently out there.

If any kind of effective change is to occur in a person's life, there must be a desire to move from worse to better. But, as Christians, we have some powerful foundational principles to guide us. First, we believe that God exists. Because He exists, we believe He has spoken. But how has He spoken? The Bible! Since He has spoken through the Bible, He has said clearly that His Word is a light unto our feet. He has given us very clear instructions on how to deal with life issues. God's way may seem odd to many people because our world has moved so far away from His ways.

Your word is a lamp to my feet and a light to my path (**Psa 119:105**).

I have chosen the way of truth; your judgments I have laid before me (**Psa 119:30**).

He sent His word and healed them, and delivered them from their destruction (**Psa 107:20**).

Your word I have hidden in my heart that I might not sin against you (**Psa 119:11**).

So shall I have an answer for him who reproaches me, for I trust in your Word. And take not the word of truth utterly out of my mouth, for I have hoped in your ordinances (**Psa 119: 42-43**).

It is through God's power and all-sufficient Word that you can find both ultimate hope and total guidance for any human problem or issue that might arise in this life. Any other solution, wrought only by human invention or wisdom, will fall far short of God's best solutions for people. I have a degree in social psychology, and as one who counseled according to it for many years, one of the consistencies I observed was the large amount of diagnoses made accompanied by little actual healing of the soul. Psychology has its benefits regarding the science of behavior. The problem comes when psychological solutions to problems are sought. Labeling is easy, and in this the solutions are often found, along with medications. What I have experienced is that they all fall far short of a good solution, especially for a Christian. I've never known anyone who used these methods to be cured, free from medications or therapy sessions. Trying to heal the soul issues of a Christian with worldly ideas will always fall far short of what God intends. The major problem is this. The world's psychiatrists and psychologists are working from a problem solving foundation that leaves out belief in sin, God, the Bible, the Holy Spirit's indwelling, grace, and Biblical forgiveness.[1] Since they do not believe in these things, their solutions must be found in creating other human solutions. I must admit, though, that for those who have rejected Christ, this is all they have. Over the years I have seen the sad results of worldly counsel. People's issues are taken care of by mere medications or some behavior modifications. These poor folks live roller-coaster lifestyles. They go from one human solution to the next until they reach a despairing death, leaving behind a path full of despair, loneliness and sadness.

The only true and lasting solution for humans is a radical change of heart through salvation. It is the total humbling of self, coming to God repentant and placing one's trust totally in Christ, desiring to be obedient to His Word in all of life's issues.

Using God's holy Word with God's people will bring hope and guidance! Why? Because God's intent is Christ-likeness and it is only through the Spirit and the Word of God and your intent to please Him that true and lasting change can occur. Thus there is a trinity of change agents: God the Spirit, the Word, and your heart's intent.

---

[1] See John MacArthur, *"The Freedom and Power of Forgiveness"* (Wheaton, Ill.: Crossway Books, 1998).

Knowing this first of all, that no prophecy of Scripture is of any private interpretation, for prophecy never came by the will of man, but holy men of God spoke as they were carried along by the agency of the Holy Spirit (**2 Pet 1:20-21**).

One of the powerful aspects of the Word of God is that it is both trans-cultural and trans-historical. It has addressed man's problems for thousands of years, in every generation of mankind. God's principles for Biblical counsel have never fluctuated as have those of psychology. The Biblical counselor has the most solid principles ever given to man-far superior to psychological solutions to human issues. The Bible has the absolute standard set down to cure soul sickness called sin and all its varied fruits of sinful thinking, feelings and actions.

For whatever things were written before were written for our learning, that we through the patience and comfort of the scriptures might have hope (**Rom 15:4**).

Because of the importance of the Scriptures, it is critical for you to learn how God thinks and what He desires for us. The more you know God's holy Word, the easier it will be to apply God's principles to your life-practice, knowing how they can guide you out of a sinful pattern of living and onto the highway of holiness and Christ-likeness.

CHANGE IS A PROCESS

All Scripture is inspired by God and profitable for teaching, for reproof, for correction, for training in righteousness (2 Tim 3:16).

Change is never an instant transformation of the whole person with no lingering issues to deal with. The process of change starts at regeneration, at which time the Holy Spirit is given by Christ to dwell within you forever. For some the process of change is slow and difficult; yet for others maturity occurs soon and Christ-likeness is strong and persevering. Why the difference? Your heart. Some have stubborn hearts that intently choose to hang on to habitual sins, even though they know that's wrong. Things like sexual lusts, anger, greed, self-centeredness, lying or deceiving, and heart idols are all things the Spirit yearns to rid you of. But because you won't intently deal with these sinful issues, spiritual growth is slow. Many times the Spirit has to use affliction to change you. It is as though the Spirit has no cooperation from you. The Spirit strives to get you to apply scriptural principles to life's issues so that you become more Christ like. At the very core of your change is your *love* for God. Anyone can measure your practical love by your desire, through your obedience to please God and not yourself.

Now by this we know that we [intimately] know Him, if we keep His commandments. He who says, ` I know Him' and does not keep His commandments is a liar and the truth is not in him. But whoever keeps His Word, truly the love of God is matured in him...He who says he abides in Him *ought himself also to walk [live/behave] just as He walked* **(1 John 2:3-6).**

Most dictionaries define the word *change* as a "systematic series of actions directed to some end." The same is true for Christians. *The goal for you is Christ-likeness, the means to that end being the Spirit and the Word.* Change is brought about by three methods:

1. *The ministry of the Word* and the application of its principles to your life in all situations, every day, every hour!
2. *The influence and power of the Spirit* indwelling you, giving you the power/ability to change. Actually, there is absolutely no reason you can't change.
3. *The intent of choosing to be obedient* to God's Word through the power of the Spirit. This is an active choice of the Christian to intently choose to be Spirit-led. All this is wrought as you deal with your difficult wife and putting on and practicing God's principles of patience, discernment and care.

Anyone who names the name of Christ and then excludes these three basic elements is totally missing God's goal for him. *Your goal is not reformation, leaving some things out of your life like drinking, drugs, immorality, even though these things should not be a part of your life. Instead you are called to an even greater plane- transformation of your nature by being born from above (John 3:3, 5). Jesus made this clear. Unless regeneration occurs, you could be the most religious person on the earth and not enter the kingdom of God.*

Not everyone who says to Me, 'Lord, Lord,' shall enter the kingdom of heaven, but he who does the will of My Father in heaven. Many will say to Me in that day, 'Lord, Lord, have we not prophesied in your Name, have we not cast out demons in Your name, and done many wonders in Your name?' And then I will declare to them, 'I never [personally] knew you; depart from Me, you who practice lawlessness! (**Matt 7:21**).

TOTAL RESTRUCTURING MEANS DEALING WITH THE SIN IN RELATION TO ALL AREAS OF LIFE.

THE SPIRIT AND THE *HIGHWAY OF HOLINESS*
The Goal: Christ-likeness

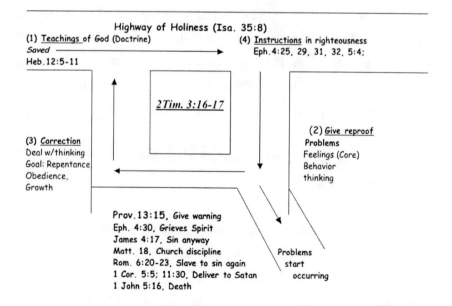

Highway of Holiness (Isa. 35:8)

(1) Teachings of God (Doctrine)
Saved
Heb. 12:5-11

(4) Instructions in righteousness
Eph. 4:25, 29, 31, 32, 5:4;

2 Tim. 3:16-17

(3) Correction
Deal w/thinking
Goal: Repentance
Obedience,
Growth

(2) Give reproof
Problems
Feelings (Core)
Behavior
thinking

Prov. 13:15, Give warning
Eph. 4:30, Grieves Spirit
James 4:17, Sin anyway
Matt. 18, Church discipline
Rom. 6:20-23, Slave to sin again
1 Cor. 5:5; 11:30, Deliver to Satan
1 John 5:16, Death

Problems
start
occurring

As you look at the illustration above, you will notice there are four important life elements: 1) the teachings of God, 2) convictions or giving reproof, 3) disciplined training through correction, and 4) instructions in righteousness. All of these are based on 2 Timothy 3:16-17 and the life cycles you will go through as you grow in Christ. Let's look at each one and explain how each operates. As you go through this, you will see that these four cycles are the very things we all go through.

A.   The Teachings of God

For real and lasting Biblical change to occur there must be acceptable change in your relationship to God. The first priority is your vertical, saving relationship with God. The result of this relationship will greatly impact your horizontal relationships, like with your wife. But the converse is also true. Unresolved relationships on the horizontal (between you and your wife) can hinder your vertical relationship with God. This has nothing to do with one's secured salvation, but your fellowship with Him that can be hindered. This can remove daily peace and contentment in your life.

"...That your prayers may not be hindered" **(1 Pet 3:7; c.f. Matt 6:14-15).**

Once your salvation is secured at your regeneration, you are placed practically on *"The highway of holiness"* in which you are taught the Word by the Spirit. You are not only taught how to biblically deal with sin issues in your life, you are taught how to "put on" and practice what is right (Matt 5:29-30; 1 Pet 4:1-5). ***This is the critical part that is usually missing in growth.*** An ever-increasing knowledge of doctrine and the practice of it should be ever-present in your life. As issues come up in your marriage, you go to the Bible (or ask your discipler) and see what God says to do in that particular situation. And as you do this over the years, you are building a strong foundation for maturity. It all starts with small building blocks of spiritual growth. True spiritual growth never happens overnight. It is a life decision to devote yourself to doing things God's way, no matter the circumstances.

B.   Conviction Of Sins

When you choose to sin with deliberate intent, you leave the highway of holiness and need reproof. I say you "leave with intent" because the unbiblical notion that people *"fall"* into sin is simply false. You intentionally choose to sin, and in that rebellion against God and His ways, you sin! Reproof can happen through several means. Ultimately, the work of the Spirit Himself comes through the Word, your God given conscience, a family member, a close friend or the church (1 Tim 5:20; Titus 1:9; James 2:9). Reproof is the first step to getting the person back on the highway of holiness.

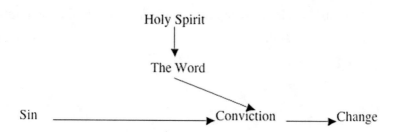

But what is the goal of conviction? It all pertains to your relationship with God. You should recognize this conviction of wrong because your fellowship with God is hindered, and God Himself requires a right relationship. In this is a picture of God's love for you. If God were to leave conviction of sin out of 2 Timothy 3:16-17, you would have nothing more than behavioral change. This is usually the goal in both secular and many integrational counseling approaches. Psychology has already ruled out sin, thereby eliminating conviction of sin. Tragically, this is one of the major influences psychology has had on the church. The church today has accepted many worldly psychological labels, thus eliminating personal responsibility for sin and true Biblical change through the integration of Scriptural principles, functionally seeing scripture as not sufficient enough to meet all the issues of life. It is important to realize that your own sin is just that, *your own sin.* No one makes you sin-not your wife, your job, or circumstances. You choose to go this direction out of ungodly intentions. You choose sin because in some sort of warped way it actually pleases your fallen nature and accomplishes your evil ends. To change, you must take full responsibility for your own thoughts, behavior, and actions. It is interesting to note that the Greek word for "conviction" is *elegchos* and is used here in 2 Timothy 3:16 and Revelation 3:19. It means "to show someone their sin and summons them to repentance." True repentance acknowledges guilt of sin. Below is a short comparison of the differences I have been discussing.

Biblical Change	Psychology/Integrational Counseling
Sin	Others fault, not responsible
Full responsibility For one's actions	Circumstances
Required change	Chemical imbalance
Conviction, repentance	No sin
Power of Spirit	Power of self-worth/esteem
Word as authority	Human wisdom
Other-oriented	My needs must be met first, then others
Romans 12:14, 17-21	

For the wisdom of this world is foolishness with God. For it is written, He taketh the wise in their own craftiness (1 Cor 3:19).

C. Correction

This is the next step after conviction has occurred in your life. For Biblical change to occur, the Scriptures are the crucial thing used to correct your life issues/sin.[2] The Scriptures have the ability to either bring affliction to your life or bring healing to the soul (Isa 30:26). The Greek word for "correction" is *epanorthosis* and means "standing up," or "making something to stand again." The Word of God has the power to correct your thinking, actions, feelings and behaviors so as to make you once again stand and go on to please God. Second Timothy 3:16 is the only place in which this word is used in the Bible. Scripture not only convicts you of your sin but

---

[2] The author recognizes that life issues might be occurring that are not sinful issues but stem from an organic problem. As a resource see '*Blame It On The Brain*' Edward Welch, P and R publishing, 1998.

helps you get out of the destructive lifestyle you are heading toward. In order for change to occur, there are four important things about correction that practically should take place in your life.

> *The first step in correction is repentance:* (metanoia *means "to rethink"*). It is a rethinking of your behavior, attitude, or beliefs to align with God's will. Nothing in it speaks of sorrow; it doesn't speak of emotions at all. There is a Greek word that carries the idea of sorrow; it is *"metamelomai,"* to express regret, remorse. It is used in Matthew 27:3 of Judas. He had tremendous sorrow or regret due to the consequences of his evil actions, not because he felt they were a sin against God. Hebrews 12:17 discusses Esau's inability to repent in spite of his emotional outburst. He had regret for the consequences of his sin, but he did not see his actions as a sin before God.

> *For godly sorrow produces repentance leading to salvation, not to be regretted, but the sorrow of the world leads to death* **(2 Cor 7:10).**

This verse above teaches that there is a "Godly sorrow" that produces repentance, which should never be confused with self-centered, ungodly regret. Esau's sorrow and Judas's regret did not lead to true repentance before God. Why? Because they would not humble themselves and seek the forgiveness of God, taking full responsibility for their actions. The apostle Peter himself denied the Lord Jesus three times yet repented and found forgiveness. He was later used of God greatly. True repentance will produce life fruit. Biblical repentance involves 3 things:

1. Confession of your sin, seeking restoration of your daily fellowship with God.
2. Seeking to forgive others as God forgives you and a willingness to make things right.
3. A turning away from that sin (putting-off) and practicing instead God's principles (putting-on).

THE KEY

True repentance is by the power of the Spirit, through the pure grace of God, in the direction of obedience to the Word of God.

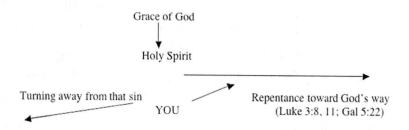

God the Spirit uses His inspired Scriptures to bring both repentance and guidance in your life. This is why you should become, over time, a theologian who can apply these principles to every life situation. So when your wife is acting mean or does something against you that is wrong, these are the very moments you must seek to learn the godly responses, based on the Word. That means you go to the Scriptures, study for an answer, and then apply it to your situation. The better you know the Scriptures, the better potential you have for change. You may be the only one in your home doing this, but you must pursue holiness, even if you're alone. The Scriptures deal with the heart, and if there is no radical change of the heart by regeneration, you can never please God and obey His Word. Learning all the psychological labels and terms matters little in comparison to knowing the Scriptures and how they apply to every situation.

The second step in correction is confession of sin and receiving forgiveness.

He who covers his sins will not prosper, but whoever confesses and forsakes them will have mercy **(Prov 28:13; see also Psa 10:13; 4, 14; Prov 20:30).**

The Hebrew word for confession is *Yaddah* and means "to throw" or "to cast." It was used of casting lots or counting votes, or to recant and tell one's side of the story in a trial. It relates to telling the facts of an event. The Greek term for confession is *"homologeo"* and means "to say the same thing." A person accused of a crime will openly agree with the pronouncement that they are guilty. This word doesn't carry the idea of a subjective acknowledgement of a crime; it is used of an open confession to others.

For you, confession is an acknowledgement of your guilt, agreeing with the conviction. Psychology may have you confess all your problems, but that is to merely unload or to express yourself. Not so with true Biblical change. It is taking responsibility for your life and aligning it to God's principles. It is taking responsibility for all the wrong you have done in your marriage. Without Biblical confession there can be no true forgiveness or reconciliation toward God. An honest and sincere person must deal with this up front before true spiritual growth can occur. There can be no more playing games, procrastination, or even worse, taking lightly the idea of eternal judgment and hell.

If we confess our sins, He is faithful and just to forgive us our sins and to cleanse us from all unrighteousness (1 **John 1:9).**

Continual recognition of sin and confession in your life is a sign that you are a true Christian. While false teachers and worldly psychologists deny even the reality of sin, this too is a sign of their unbelief and lostness. Yet, many Christians go to these very people for help and guidance. They might as well go to a witch doctor or the local bum on the street. Anyone's view counts at this point. Their sole authority is not based on the Word of God, but on one's experiences, subjective hunches and ideas. That's why there are so many psychological models in the world. Each psychologist takes from this pool of human ideas and creates his or her own view. When David was walking in his sin, he said:

When I kept silent, my bones grew old, through my groaning all the day long. For day and night Your hand was heavy upon me; my vitality was turned into the drought of summer. But I acknowledged my sin to You, and my iniquity I have not hidden. I shall say, 'I confess my transgression to the Lord,' and you forgave the iniquity of my sin. For this cause everyone who is godly shall pray to You in a time when You may be found (Psa 32:3-6).

Due to psychology's total denial of sin, and Christ's sacrifices, psychological counselees remain and grope in their sin. These poor people seek solutions that ultimately will fail. Medications, undealt with sin, and a lack of regeneration will only bring more misery, bankrupt lives and eternal damnation. Instead of confession to a very loving, forgiving, and merciful God, they will be directed to medication, blame-shifting, or morbid introspection. Their lives may have times of limited peace, but little true peace and lasting solutions. I have seen this countless times. Such people go from one counselor to the next, spending a lot of money with little results. They seem to never come to the truth, struggling to find an empty hope, spiraling down until death. Men like Freud, Rogers, Skinner, Maslo, along with all the other counseling systems, offer no other way of dealing effectively with the reality of sin, not realizing that we all live in a moral universe created by a moral God. In that moral universe, every sinful action will have its moral consequence, if not now then later. What we see today in many people's lives is the reaction of this through strange behavior, suicide, deep depression, drug addiction, and lives filled with turmoil. Never able to find lasting solutions to their problems.

If we say that we have no sin, we deceive ourselves, and the truth is not in us (**1 John 1:8**).

And many shall follow their pernicious ways; by reason of whom the way of truth shall be evil spoken of (**2 Pet 2:2**).

For if we sin willfully after we have received the knowledge of the truth, there remains no more sacrifice for sins (**Heb 10:26**).

Ever learning, and never able to come to the knowledge of the Truth (**2 Tim 3:7**).

The third step in correction is the forsaking of sin. The Hebrew word for this means "to let go, putting off." God repeatedly calls you to forsake sin and follow His ways because they are always the best. This "letting go" is the same as the Biblical principle of putting off sin from your life. This process of putting off involves four heart elements.

1. **Heart desire to deny self and say no to sin and to self-centered desires.** By choosing to sin intently, you are functionally saying that sin is more important and valuable than Christ.

2. **Forsaking sin is a conscious choice of breaking with the sinful habits of the past.** This could involve people, places, or situations. It is building up guards to help protect you. It is making yourself accountable to others. One of my counselees is a good example of this. Jose was a young man who struggled with pornography. A few guards were set-up to effectively help him forsake it. Like not driving past the local strip bar on the way home from work, instead taking a different route. Removing the porn cable channels from his TV. Ultimately, though, he had to realize that along with these helpful external guards, the real issue was his heart.

Jose had to desire, out of his love for God, to please Him above all else.

3. **Learning to train and retrain your imagination and thinking to be biblically oriented, capturing by intent every thought to Christ.**

And do not be conformed to this world, but be transformed by the renewing of your mind, that you may prove what is that good and acceptable and perfect will of God (**Rom 12:2**).

The fourth step in correction is restoration: Once you have repented of your sin(s) and are habitually walking by the Word, restoration is part of the forgiveness process (2 Cor 2:7). Restoration is not only with God, but to others you have offended (Matt 5:23-24).

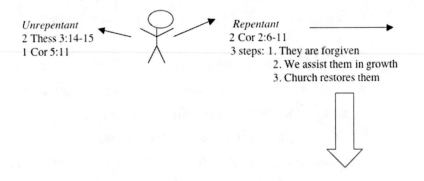

Unrepentant
2 Thess 3:14-15
1 Cor 5:11

Repentant
2 Cor 2:6-11
3 steps: 1. They are forgiven
2. We assist them in growth
3. Church restores them

THE ONE CRITICAL MISSING PIECE

D. Disciplined training (instruction) in righteousness

Now we come to the fourth part in our *"highway of holiness"*. First we had the teachings of God, then the conviction of sin. Thirdly we had correction. Now we come to the forth and most crucial of all life actions, the disciplined training in righteousness. The word *"training"* here in 2 Timothy 3:16, is used many times of training a child. The Greek word is *paideia*. It is also used in Ephesians 6:4 *"But bring them up with the Lord's training and counsel (nouthesia)."* There is always a two-sided approach to training. Training and counsel go hand and hand. Training is used this way in Proverbs 29:15- *the rod (training) and rebuke (counsel).* It is structured discipline, the use of reward and punishment. ***The Hebrew word* Masar *is used for instruction; it is instruction by chastening which should result in education.*** It is also used in Hebrews 12:5-11, where chastisement (or discipline) that is unpleasant when administered is said to result in 'a peaceful fruit of righteousness to those who have been trained by it." In verse 11 it is related to the painful training of an athlete.

> *If you endure chastening, God deals with you as sons; for what son is there whom a father does not chasten? But if you are without chastening, of which all have become partakers, then you are illegitimate and not sons. Furthermore, we have had human fathers who corrected us, and we paid them respect. Shall we not much more readily in subjection to the Father of spirits and live?...Now no chastening seems to be joyful for the present, but painful; nevertheless, afterward it yields the peaceable fruit of righteousness to those who have been trained by it.*

The questions are often asked, *"If God forgave me of my sin, what more does He want? What does this training in righteousness have to do with reward and punishment? Why is there this additional part?"* You must understand that forgiveness of your sin means that God will no longer hold it against you. You have been justified with Him through faith in Christ and His work on the Cross on your behalf. In your place, He took the wrath of God upon Himself that you actually deserved. That was a one-time act. Now the progressive action of sanctification is a daily part of your life. The indwelling Spirit gives you the power to carry out the Word, helping you to overcome temptations. Now God is concerned about your future condition. If there is no training in righteousness, no athletic pursuit of righteousness and holiness in your daily life, those same sins will be back. He is trying to spare you from the disappointment of failure with the same sins over and over.

Effecting Biblical Change: The Highway of Holiness

THE CENTRAL KEY TO LASTING CHANGE

In all the years I've been ministering to men who have difficult wives, the problem has usually been that they live within the first three cycles on the highway of holiness but not within the fourth one, the actual *training in righteousness*. You must realize there are four steps, not just three, if you are going to have effective, biblical change in your life. God the Spirit gave all four steps to give you direction over the power of sin and all its destructive methods and spiritual growth. The put-off/put-on method is essential in dealing with sin. The Christian life is more than just stopping to sin in an area. It must include the "putting on of righteousness" in all areas and striving to keep them in place like an athlete would.

For God did not call us to uncleanness, but in holiness (1 Thess 4:7).

Pursue peace with all people [this means your wife], and holiness, without which no one will see the Lord (Heb 12:14).

As you read this book, I'm presupposing you're in a difficult situation. You have been continually suffering with this hardship concerning your wife and nothing seems to work. Going to church more, trying "to be spiritual," has usually ended up in failure, both with you and your family. You have chosen sin, received reproof and correction continually, but training in righteousness is the one thing you have not committed yourself too continually over the long haul. The picture looks like this.

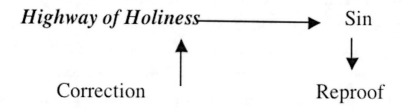

Can this one missing piece create a deadly cycle? Yes! A disciplined, athletic desire to strive in your life, through the power of the Spirit, to actually pursue holiness and Christ-likeness is usually the one missing element that can eventually cause apathy and spiritual declension. There simply is no habitual spiritual training in your life. You have seen the first three steps and been through them many times, always learning but with no real growth or endurance.

The fourth step is essentially putting off habitual sins and putting on habitually righteous ways within one's life daily, in every situation-at work, play, home, and with your difficult wife. Putting off alone will not bring about spiritual growth. It is the actual putting on and practicing, through the power of the Spirit and obedience to the Word that brings real and lasting growth (see Eph 4; Col 3). *Putting off habitual sins alone leaves a vacuum that will again be filled. That filling will eventually be those same habitual sins unless the putting on of biblical ways is done.*

RIGHEOUSNESS THE GOAL

How is righteousness attained in disciplined training? This is not the same kind of righteousness that is imputed or given to you at your salvation through the work of Christ (Rom 3:22; 5:19). The righteousness that Paul is referring to here in 2 timothy 3:16 is different. What Paul is referring to in Romans 3:22 is the righteousness through justification, something you cannot earn or deserve. *But in 2 Timothy it is the righteousness of sanctification.* The first is your standing before God; the second is the actual righteousness that takes place in your life daily. This righteousness of sanctification is empowered by the Spirit through your intention to choose right. Biblically, both kinds of righteousness are joined, which creates the potential for real spiritual growth.

The second righteousness comes from the Greek word that means "rightness, straightness." *Righteousness is conformity to God's biblical standard.* Because we are made right in our vertical relationship with God the Father, we are now to intently pursue righteousness in our horizontal relationships. This certainly includes the relationship with your wife. She may not want to be at peace with you, but you can be at peace with her through Christ.

Pursue peace with all people and holiness, without which no one will see the Lord (Heb 12:14).

Justification is a one-time event, occurring at your regeneration. That is when God declares you right before Him, removing from you His judgment and wrath because of your faith in Christ and repentance from sin. Sanctification is that ongoing process by which, through the work of the Holy Spirit directs us toward obedience. Through the Word of God, He is molding you, reshaping you toward Christ-likeness, all of which is the very best.

True sanctification is when you daily submit in faith and obedience to the *"disciplined training"* in righteousness.

Finally, there is laid up for me the crown of righteousness, which the Lord, the righteous judge, will give me on that day, and not only me only but also to all who loved His appearing (2 Tim 4:8).

How can you pursue righteousness if there is still sin in your life?

Righteous behavior is possible, not fully as Christ was but to a much greater degree than your old sinful nature would prefer. In other words, as a Christian you should be walking in righteousness more than your sinful nature exhibits. Because you have been set free from the slavery of sin (Rom 6:20, 22), you now belong to a new master called to the task of pursuing holiness and righteousness. Pursuing holiness takes intention of heart and mind. It will never happen by osmosis.

> *Therefore since Christ suffered for us in the flesh, arm yourself also with the same mind, for he who has suffered in the flesh has ceased from sin, that he no longer should live the rest of his time in the flesh for the desires of men, but for the will of God (1 Pet 4:1-2).*

The passage above says several things to us about our battle with sin and how to overcome it.

1. Before your salvation, you were a slave to sin and all that you did was of the flesh; in fact, you had no choice but to naturally walk in sin. But things have been radically changed and you are now a slave to Christ. Because you are united with Christ, the issue of slavery to sin is broken.
2. Whenever you are tempted, there is a battle between your flesh and your renewed spirit. That is a sign not to fall into passivity or apathy, but to rise up and arm yourself through the Spirit and the Word.
3. With Christ, you can overcome. You will never be tempted beyond what you can take (1 Cor 10:13).
4. It is possible to live the rest of your life doing and growing into more righteousness, due to the power of the Spirit within you and a true desire to be obedient to His word.

Righteousness is a possibility for all Christians, not total but ever-increasing. You will continue to be tempted by the flesh, the world and Satan, but victories can be yours. *"The Lord knows how to deliver the godly out of temptations" (2 Pet 2:9).* Because of your regeneration, you now have the ability to choose righteousness over sin. Your task is to choose intently righteous behavior over sinful behavior. You are to grow in your life to become what you are positionally in Christ. You are dead to yourself and have been resurrected to live for Christ (Rom 6:5-11).

Slavery to sin   You   Slave to Christ

CHAPTER THREE

Your Life-God's Glory

THE ULTIMATE GOAL: GOD'S GLORY, NOT YOUR WIFE

Even though this book is about how husbands can develop a biblical strategy for dealing with wives who are bitter, angry and difficult to live with, the ultimate motivations and intents of a man's actions and thoughts must be for the glory of God. Everything in world events, all the occurrences throughout life, are there in order to somehow bring glory to God. It's much like why God saved you. You were doomed to hell, and well deserving of it. The Bible says all have sinned and fallen short of what God desires (Rom 3:23), so why would God have a strategy to save you? Why would He even plan your salvation before time itself?

Just as He chose us in Him before time began, that we should be holy and without blame before Him **(Eph 1:4).**

Therefore, whether you eat or drink, or whatever you do, do all to the glory of God **(1 Cor 10:31).**

Not because you are of some sort of worth to God or that you are just so good that somehow you deserve heaven. Never! No one ever born could do anything themselves to merit heaven (Rom 9:11). God did all this for one purpose, as with all He does, for His glory, not yours. You could not see the divine attributes of mercy, love and forgiveness in the creation apart from God's salvation through Christ and the cross. All of these things point to His glory and your worship of Him.

You may be asking at this point, *"I thought this was to win my wife back and have a good marriage?"* No, I can promise no man that this strategy will win her back or that your marriage will be great. I do hope that as a man puts into practice these biblical principles that his wife would come to repentance. I remember a couple who came for counseling at church. The man's name was Chuck. He was a seminary student and looking toward the pastorate. He was a very intelligent, handsome and sincere person who really loved the Lord and wanted to serve Him. After three years of marriage, his wife told him she no longer loved him and within a short time moved out and divorced him. She refused any counseling and apparently had her own agenda, not God's. Here was a sincere man who could do nothing but wave good-bye to his wife. He dropped out of seminary and decided to get a full-time job in the business world.

Proverbs 13:15 says, *"The way of the unfaithful is hard."* After Chuck's former wife chose to disobey God and His divine principles and do what she wanted, her life became hard and to this day trouble, bad relationships, and difficult times have followed her. She is much worse off than before. He, on the other hand, chose to remain faithful to God and His principles. Even though his heart was saddened, he remained steadfast and faithful. In his life, a hope and peace surrounded him that only God could give. He also learned many things through this situation and was able to help other men. He is a man living for God's glory, not his own.

A Christian man's goal in life should not be to make a lot of money, have a lot of toys, or even have a perfect marriage (even though we do hope for this), rather it should be to glorify God in his daily life, his actions, his thinking, and how he treats others. The fruits of all this will be holiness and peace and perhaps a good marriage. The man's goal is to, *"Seek first the kingdom of God, then all these things will be added [Subjunctive: Conditioned upon God's will] to your life."* Your calling is to minister to your wife, realizing that no matter how mean, insensitive, or sinful she may act, you can remain steadfast, faithful, loving, and yet discerning in all situations. You can be a man of God, a man of integrity, a man who seeks to glorify God, even in a difficult marriage.

You're much like what we talked about earlier. In the midst of battles, when your kids are disrespecting, your wife is being greedy and wasteful with your hard earned money, even in the midst of complaining, you actually can stand calm, at peace, and steadfast in living out biblical principles. You know several important things: God is in total control; He is there close to you, strengthening you because ***"all things will work together for good to those who love the Lord and are called according to His will" (Rom 8:28).*** That itself brings great comfort. But if your wife chooses to walk in habitual sin, even for many years and toss aside the peace of God in her own life, their is little you can do except walk in holiness and be that godly example of both Word and action in her life.

And the peace of God, which surpasses all understanding, will guard your hearts and minds through Christ Jesus (Phil 4:7).

In the verse above, Paul wrote about this peace in the midst of tremendous hardship and surrounded by people full of hate toward him. His mere focus, in the midst of life's battles, remained while doing what was right, no matter how he felt. No matter the turmoil around him, he could have God's peace in his life. Paul was probably in a Roman prison (60-62 AD) and writing this from there. The conditions were not easy and antagonism was great, yet he had peace. But what is this peace Paul had? It is an inner calm or tranquility that is promised to believers who have a thankful attitude, based on their unwavering confidence that God is able and willing to do what is best for them, even in the midst of turmoil. You too can have this same peace. It's much like the Scripture that says there was peace at the cross:

For it pleased the Father that in Him all the fullness should dwell, and by Him to reconcile all things to Himself, by Him, whether things on the earth or things in heaven, having made peace through the blood of His cross (Col 1:19-20).

How was there peace at the cross? There were men filled with hate yelling at Christ. There was lightening, an earthquake, and death. Yet there was peace at the cross. How? Because Christ, the Son of God, was doing God the Father's will, paying the penalty for the sins of all, to those who would believe. The term *"blood"* is an expression of the totality of Christ's atoning sacrifice for sins, His death (see Eph 1:7; 2:13; Heb 9:14; 1 Pet 1:19). Because of this there could be peace for believers in the midst of great turmoil, just as there can be in your life, in the midst of a difficult marriage. You can have peace in your daily walk, not by ignoring your problems or even running away from them, but by seeking to glorify God in all you do, say, and think. This needs to be your primary focus in daily life. *You must rise above the situation and see things from a higher plane, as Christ did. See the big picture, not the one snapshot of the moment.*

As you commit yourself to daily prayer, Bible reading and study, memorizing scripture and striving to be obedient to God's principles in all areas of your life, there will be victory. I can't promise victory in your wife's life, because you're the one reading the book. But I can promise you these other things. If you don't do what is right, taking to heart your daily walk with the Lord, according to His principles and having a desire to please Him, trouble, confusion and great despair will plague you for many years.

FOCUSING ON THE NEW EARTH, NOT THE OLD
A GREAT HOPE

But the Day of the Lord will come as a thief in the night, in which the heavens will pass away with a great noise, and the elements will melt with fervent heat; both the earth and the works that are in it will be burned up (2 Pet 3:10).

Now I saw a new heaven and a new earth, for the first heaven and the first earth had passed away. Also there was no sea. Then I, John, saw the holy city, New Jerusalem,

> *coming down out of heaven from God, prepared as a bride*
> *adorned for her husband (Rev 21:1-2).*

Your focus in life many times sets the pace and mood for your lifestyle. So many men I have known and counseled are so wrapped up in today's problems and lack of hope for change in their wife that life seems bleak. They walk about everyday like men who want to do one of two things: either just die and go to heaven, or go away from the situation all together and move out of the home. If you are one of those men reading this book, you may have felt one or both of these ways many times. Just awhile ago a friend of mine said, *"My wife is so hard to live with I'm fed up and feel like saying good-bye and moving out."* This man is a Christian working at a Christian institution, yet living a life that is filled with hardship and only spurts of occasional joy.

Let me tell you a true story about someone I know personally. His name is Jim. He grew up in a home where there were no Christians. At an early age he came to know Christ and this affected his life greatly. He grew up in a local church and was very faithful to the Lord and certain ministries. He went to a Christian college and seminary and eventually came to minister in a church in southern California. God blessed his teaching ministry in many ways and hundreds of lives were greatly changed because of his faithfulness and love for the Lord. Then Jim met a Christian lady in the church and eventually married her. The first couple years were good, but after several years she started to become very embittered and angry due to her own sinful desires. For many years after their marriage, their lives were filled with arguments, a few separations, and a lot of bleak days for Jim. He really wanted to serve the Lord, but he knew he had to work on his marriage first in order to be biblically qualified to minister. So for ten years he stayed out of ministry, got a job and worked on himself and his marriage. He tried all kinds of ways to improve his marriage, but everything seemed to fail and his marriage changed very little. After ten years Jim finally realized that his goals were all wrong. He had focused so much on his wife and pleasing her that he lost his true focus on what God wanted him to become, even in the midst of turmoil. This seed thought hit him hard. It was from this that he began to study his Bible from a different perspective. Now he was studying it for himself to learn how God wanted him to think and act. He was not studying just from the perspective of teaching others. The teacher needed to be taught from God's Word.

Jim spent years reading and learning the principles from God's Word on how to treat those who hate you, how to take every thought captive, how to desire God's will and not just his own, and most of all, he realized this life is short when compared to the life he will have on the new earth, forever. Since, as Christians, we have died to selfish desires and been resurrected to live for Christ, he realized that he needs to focus on the betterment of others and not just himself. This meant his wife also. To see that our way, our desires and our perspective are not as important than the holiness for our wife and her sanctification or salvation. Bank accounts, cars, clothing, houses or anything else should never be a priority for a man who is a Christian. When you realize you're dead to self and have been made alive to Him, your whole reaction to your wife and situations will change to honor God.

This life is only a stopover to greater things to come. What God wants you to do is remain faithful to Him and the situation you are in now. This marriage did not take God by surprise. He knew all about it. It's interesting to note that the most important thing to God when it comes to His awesome big picture is not your situation, even though that's important to Him. It's not your physical body or health, even though God does care about these things. Then what is it? The real you! Your human Spirit, that part of you that will live forever, either in heaven or hell; one of those two places and no other. Let me explain. The real you, that part of you reading this book, grasping what I'm writing, is your human Spirit. That part of you God imparted at conception. Your physical body is a tool God created to help move you around on this earth.

God's priority for the real you is primarily, as a Christian, to make you Christ-like in all your ways, all your thinking, and all your actions in how you treat others, even those who don't like you. *He is in the process of preparing you for how things will be on the new earth.* He brings in things to help you react according to His Word, allowing you to grow spiritually. The more you rebel against this process, the longer and harder it will be for you to become Christ-like.

The choices you make as a Christian affect your growth. Most humans are stubborn and few really desire to fully grow to be Christ-like, especially in the hard areas of life, regarding money, power, sex, view of self, or pride. God has to bring hardship into their lives in order to break their stubbornness and conform the real them into Christ-likeness.

This long hardship does two things. Either they finally give in and are broken, yielding to God's principles, or they choose to despair even more, making things worse for themselves. I have found that many men choose the second way, even as Christians, because they simply do not want to practice God's principles in their life and situation. They see them as to hard and requiring to much change. They also may have failed to study God's Word for answers and are thus honestly ignorant of what to do. That's one of the reasons I wrote this book-to give men some Biblical instruction on how to deal with difficult marriage situations.

So many men are myopic, going through life as through a tunnel, not seeing or understanding the big picture God has for each of them. They are so wrapped up in their own hardships that they can't see outside the box. Let me share with you the big picture.

YOUR FINAL DESTINY

Now I saw a new heaven and a new earth, for the first heaven and the first earth had passed away (Revelations 21:1)

One day when Christ comes back, believers will be removed from the earth. From this point onward the hard times, called the Tribulation, hit the earth. Once all the Biblical end-times events are completed, God is going to burn up the entire universe, all the stars, all the planets, including the earth. Everything you have cherished here on earth will be destroyed. All the former bank accounts, homes, cars, clothing, everything will be gone. Then God is going to make a new earth. Quite larger than the older one. There will be no sun, no oceans, and a new city will be put there called the New Jerusalem. All believers in Christ will be placed on the new earth and we will be there forever. No aging, no sickness or death, and no marriage problems will exist. It will be a restored Eden without the serpent. You will have a new body that will live forever. Your view of things will be crystal clear and sharp, In fact, the former life will have seemed like a thick fog when compared to your new existence. Your human Spirit, the real you, is now fully conformed to Christ and existing in an immortal body, similar in looks to your former body because others will recognize you. Everything you think, say and do will be in perfect harmony with what God was trying to teach you back on the old earth. Take a few moments to think about this awesome reality, that this is really going to happen to you. It's not some story or made-up theory; God has already planned it out, and all is going too happen just as He wills, and you're a part of that plan.

When you grasp the big picture, your small situation should not appear to be so awesome and horrific after all. It's a minor scene in a very long movie. Only this movie is the big reality show. And your part is to act Christ-like in this situation with a wife who is not walking by the Spirit or obeying God's Word. What God wants you to do is trust Him, love Him, and follow Him daily in your growth. He has given you salvation, regeneration, the Spirit to empower you to carry out the Word of God in your life, and a glimpse of what is to come. You can know as Moses knew that he was only a sojourner on this earth; this was not his true home. Therefore he sacrificed all he had to pursue God and His ways. Be as Moses, who could have been a powerful and rich prince of the super power of that day, Egypt. Yet he chose to follow God and His ways.

By faith, Moses, when he became of age, refused to be called the son of Pharaoh's daughter, choosing rather to suffer affliction with the people of God than to enjoy the passing pleasures of sin, esteeming the reproach of Christ greater riches than the treasures in Egypt, for he looked forward (Heb 11:24-26).

Therefore we do not lose heart. Even though our outward man is perishing, yet the inward man is being renewed day by day. For our light affliction, which is but for a moment, is working for us a far more exceeding and eternal weight of glory, while we do not look at the things which are seen, but the things which are not seen. For the things which are seen are temporary, but the things which are not seen are eternal (2 Cor 4:16-18).

WHAT EVER HAPPENED TO STEVE AND MIKE

Steve started off having many struggles and trials and things didn't change overnight for him. It took several years of being consistent with both his walk with the Lord and his wife to even start seeing changes in his marriage. Eventually his wife saw this change in Steve's life and began to examine her own walk with the Lord and sought biblical counseling also. Today their marriage is an example too many in their church of how it should be. Both bringing glory to God through their lives together. Mikes story though didn't turn out this way. Mike did continue to grow in the Lord and sought to please Him in all he did. Through this affliction he grew stronger. He was in no way perfect but he was striving to apply God's principles in his life and marriage. His wife though had other desires that were directed in ways that would meet her own plans. To her, peace, love and fulfillment were found in another man in Arizona and eventually blamed Mike for all her problems, seeing herself as a victim. She moved out, divorced Mike and moved in with her boyfriend. She still claimed to be a Christian and told us,"*God wanted her to be happy, that she finally found a man she could love.*" Mike sought to make things right with his wife but she had her sights on other things. She eventually found a so called 'Christian counselor' to agree with her and told her "it was ok to divorce her husband. That God wants her happy." Today Mike is doing fine in his life as he faithfully serves in our church and as you talk to him, he is a man full of peace and contentment. He found this in following after God's ways no matter how he felt or his past circumstances.

CHAPTER FOUR

The Power To Being Different

The last question you may be asking is, *"How can I be this way. After all, I've been living this bad way all my life?"* When you became a Christian several important things occurred in your life. One of the most critical blessings God has given you, besides your salvation, is the very presence of His Spirit dwelling within you. The Holy Spirit gives you the power (ability)[3] to actually carry out God's Word in your own difficult situation. Let's take a look at what the Spirit's presence means in your life and what He can do for you in the midst of turmoil. This is all part of the sanctification process. [4]As I shared this with Mike and Steve, their awareness of God's indwelling presence changed what they thought and did everyday of their lives.

The Personal Work Of The Spirit In Your Life

The personal work of the Spirit in a man's life appears to be one of the silent teachings in the church. *Most believers are not aware of the Spirit's daily work in their lives and when a man is*

---

[3] The Greek word is *dunymis* and means having the ability to do something.
[4] See *The Biblical Anthology On The Spirit Of God*, p 338.

walking in sin, He grieves the Spirit within. He can be grieved by their apathy toward real spiritual growth, and He is hindered by their laziness and selfishness in letting Him guide their decisions.

It has been my personal experience in ministering to believers that for a person to actually grow in Christ-likeness there needs to be an active, conscious desire for the control/influence of the Holy Spirit over their will, emotions, and reasoning faculties. As one scholar once said, the Holy Spirit is a gentleman. He (unlike demons with the lost) will not take total control over the believer forcefully, but He does desire the very best for each believer and to lead them to godly obedience in His Word. Let's take a detailed look at the Spirit's work in the believer's life of sanctification. I do realize that there are those times when the Spirit comes crashing in on a person's life to bring about repentance, but it has been my personal experience that the Spirit is a very patient, quiet and gentle person concerning sanctification. He fully understands your hardship, difficulties and your wife. He is God and has ways that will lead you in the right direction. Let's face it, if you call yourself a Christian, doesn't it make sense that since He is God and wrote the scriptures, that you do what they say? Anything else would be sin.

The Spirit regenerated you.

I say to you, unless one is born again, he cannot see the kingdom of God... Unless one is born of water [The Word of God] and the Spirit [The Holy Spirit], He cannot enter the kingdom of God (John 3:3; 5).

Jesus here explains how one is born again. It is interesting to note that the actual Greek says, *"born from above,"* One is regenerated *"from above"* because that is where salvation starts. This is referring to your election before time began.

Your salvation started from above, heaven, where God is. Titus 3:5 brings this out forcefully. The Spirit and Word are the two ingredients necessary in bringing about this salvation: *"He saved us through the washing of regeneration and renewing of the Holy Spirit."*

Salvation brings about this divine cleansing (like water) from sin and gives the gift of a new Spirit-generated, Spirit-empowered life as God's children. This is part of what Jesus talked about with Nicodemus in John 3. This means that you were regenerated and made a new person. Even though you have been acting like your old self, you must repent and choose to put into practice the principles of God in your life. To Mike and Steve, the light seemed to come on when they realized this spiritual reality that occurred in their lives. The big problem was their lack of awareness and disciplined training in righteousness. As Christians, they had been so trained all their lives in walking in the flesh that it came so natural. Lying, cheating, lusting and anger seemed to be the natural thing to do as a human because it takes little effort. But as they began to realize what they were actually doing to their Savior, the Holy Spirit and those around them, the walls of hardness around their hearts started to break apart. For most people I work with, this is usually the start of many changes in their lives. It was here that Mike and Steve started repenting and becoming very acutely aware of their sins. And in doing all this they became better able to handle their difficult wives. They could actually walk by the Spirit, even amongst the turmoil in the home, giving out wise counsel, staying calm and peaceful. That will be a shocker to any wife.

The Spirit indwells you permanently

The New Testament clearly teaches that when a person puts his faith in Christ as Messiah and repents before God, the Spirit comes in to dwell permanently in the new believer's life.

There is therefore now no condemnation to those who are in Christ Jesus, who do not walk according to the flesh, but according to the Spirit (Rom 8:11).

In 1 Corinthians 3:16, the actual Greek translation reads: *"Know you not that a shrine of God you are and the Spirit God in you dwells."*

In these verses above, the Holy Spirit wants you to know how central the issues are concerning what the Trinity has done in saving and sanctifying you. He wants you *'to know'*. All believers should fully understand and grasp this reality. We are not to forget it or be unaware. Next, the Spirit wrote in these verses that you are *'a shrine'*. The Greek word used is not a large temple; instead it is the word *'naos'.* This word means the inner room of the Holy of Holies. Because of the Spirit dwelling within you, God Himself, that very presence makes you Holy. It is not due to anything within you, but through the work of Christ on your behalf. The word *'dwells'* carries the idea of down or permanence. The indwelling Spirit is there to remain permanent in you, never to leave or depart. Even if you sin or chose for awhile to live in habitual sin, you will grieve the Spirit within you (Ephesians 4:30); this illustrates the idea of divine emotion. The Spirit is striving within you to prompt you to go in the right way, the best way, and He sees you intently choosing a way that is harmful and disastrous; both to you and others around you, this grieves Him. Because of our rebelliousness, we will face the discipline of the Lord in our lives through different afflictions that will occur in order to bring about a sincere repentance and purity. This whole verse brings out the fact that *"you are"* a shrine because of the very presence of God within you. But, because of your choice to intently sin, your shrine is defiled, (Temple) because of the way you have been acting towards your difficult situation, but God the Spirit wants you to put on Christ's principles and walk in a manner worthy of your calling.

I, Therefore, the prisoner of the Lord, beseech you to walk worthy of the Calling with which you were called, with all lowliness and gentleness, with longsuffering bearing with one another in love, endeavoring to keep the unity of the Spirit in the bond of peace (Eph 4:1-3).

Before Steve came to counseling, everything in his life came crashing down. His marriage was terrible, his job was in jeopardy and all his finances seemed to go array. Nothing positive was happening to Steve except for the fact he blamed God for all his troubles and his wife. His prayers seemed empty, no desire to worship God or read his bible. Anger, frustration and eventually depression filled his life. He also felt trapped, as if there was no way out of his wife's difficult ways. He couldn't divorce her because he knew that wasn't God's way. He felt helpless in having any kind of influence toward change in his wife's life. His view became very myopic, narrow and no real answers of hope. It's been my experience over the years that most Christians, sadly to say, must go through hardships before they are broken, broken to the point of realizing God is not to blame, only them and their sins. This is where Steve was confronted with his sins and the reality of all his terrible, selfish behavior toward his God and family. Eventually he came to realize it was his own fault for not growing in Christ. It was also at this point that Steve understood not only his position in Christ but his responsibility as a temple to strive for holiness and purity in all he does in life. When anyone comes to this reality it usually shocks them to seriousness about their daily walk with the Lord, even with a difficult wife.

He baptized you into the body of Christ at salvation

For by one Spirit we were all baptized (placed into) one body (1 Cor 12:13).

The Greek word for "baptize" basically means *"to place into."* This word was used of ships being placed into the ocean, or of dishes being submerged into water for cleansing. [5] According to this passage, the Spirit at conversion placed you into the body of Christ. Biblically there are two parts to the body of Christ, the physical and the spiritual. The spiritual body is occupied by those who have passed on and are now in heaven where they are awaiting the final consummation. The others are those who are physically alive on this earth, those who have been born-again and have the Spirit dwelling in them permanently. This was divinely planned before the foundations of the world.

This term *"baptism of the Spirit"* is not referring to water baptism, which is an outward sign, done after conversion, signifying an internal change of regeneration. Water baptism symbolizes

---

[5] Kenneth S. Wuest, *Studies in the Vocabulary of the Greek New Testament.* (Grand Rapids: Eerdmans, 1945).

Christ's death and resurrection, along with our outward testimony of our commitment to follow Christ (Rom. 6:3-5). The Spirit's placing you into the body of Christ, however emphasizes the unity of all saints throughout history. Baptism of the Spirit is not something that you should seek after in your walk with the Lord; it is already a factual reality. At your conversion you were placed into the body of Christ, given a spiritual gift (s), in order to minister to others in the body of Christ. This term *"baptism of Spirit"* is used by many teachers to refer to the constant, life-long giving of the Spirit for empowerment. But this is far from what the Scripture teaches. After Acts 2, this expression is never used of the giving of the Spirit. Instead, the key term for the Spirit's being given at conversion is *"anoint."* Believers are anointed by Jesus upon conversion, with the Spirit, once and for all (Rom 6:3-5; 8:9; Col 2:12). The Spirit is a divine person. Therefore at salvation you receive a person, fully and wholly, not a power source that can be drained like a battery and used up. You have God dwelling within you. This should cause a huge awareness within our lives toward a greater accountability and responsibility.

He guides you.

When Mike came to get help for all his problems at our church he had no direction as a Christian. He felt totally helpless, as if he could do nothing to overcome this difficult situation. As we began to work with Mike he came to the awareness that the Holy Spirit guides him through the word He wrote. That it was through the power of the Spirit in carrying out the principles of the Word that gave Mike direction in these difficult situations. It was through the word that the Spirit guides.

In John 14:26; 16:13; Jesus taught His disciples that the Spirit will assure inspirational accuracy in memory and the writing of Scripture. Because the Spirit worked in completing the Scripture, He guides believers in daily obedience. It's not through personal/ verbal revelation in which He actually speaks to them, because the canon of Scripture has been closed.

However, when He, the Spirit of truth, has come, He will guide you into all Truth; for He will not speak on His own authority, but whatever He hears He will speak; and He will tell you things to come **(John 16:13).**

But the Helper, the Holy Spirit, whom the Father will send in My name, He will teach you all things, and bring to your remembrance all things that I said to you **(John 14:26).**

If God did actually speak to someone, it should be added to the Bible because God spoke it! But the Scriptures are clear that no one is to add anything new to the Word (Deut. 4:2; 2 Cor. 4:2; 2 Pet. 3:16). We cannot even grasp fully all the Scriptures God has already given us. A scholar can spend his whole life studying the Word and never grasp everything God has revealed. Why would you want more? The Bible is clear that God has orchestrated several methods of guidance.

The Spirit uses the Word of God. He also gave you the power/ ability to carry out the Word in your life. Because of this, you are a powerhouse to do God's will. You should not be seeking some kind of subjective or mystical experience. You already have the complete counsel of God to give you everything you will ever need to know in this life. The problem for most people is that they don't like the instruction or guidance God gives. It goes directly against their selfish desires. This is why you may have some of your present problems. We all live in a moral universe because the Creator of it is a moral being. Therefore, there is a consequence to every action. If you choose to sin, there may be problems that have to be dealt with.

The Spirit gives you illumination of Scriptures. Only Spirit-filled believers have the special ability to read, understand, and carry out the Word of God. As you read the Word daily, you can grasp its meaning and have the desire to apply it to your life, no matter how you personally feel, think, or believe. God's Word should supersede all of what you want as you acquire the desire to do what God wants. Sometimes you may have acted as if what you wanted was first and that the directions God gave you were not too important. The truth is God's way is always first, the best!

That the God of our Lord Jesus Christ, the Father of Glory, may give to you the Spirit of wisdom and revelation in the knowledge of him, the eyes of your understanding being illuminated, that you may know what is the hope of His calling (Eph 1:17-18).

The Spirit sanctifies you. The word *sanctified* means to be set apart for a holy purpose. Since you should be putting to death daily the deeds of the flesh and living for Christ, this *setting apart* is meant to be for His sake. All your work, thoughts, motives, and desires are to be for Him. This in itself points you in the direction you should go. All your daily decisions are to be for the glory of God, never for your own glory.

He uses other mature believers in the church. These other mature believers have been walking by the Spirit in obedience to the Word of God for many years, and they can help disciple another toward maturity. This is why it is not good for any believer to be alone and not connected to a local body of believers. The Bible teaches that it is not good to be alone. God made us all social beings, but the problem will come when a man desires aloneness due to his problems with his wife. These are the times he needs friendships and accountability.

> *A man who isolates himself sees his own desire, he rages against all wise judgment* (**Prov 18:1**).

> *It is not good that a man should be alone* (**Gen 2:18**).

You need fellowship, accountability and teaching. One of the main reasons people don't pursue these is because there are things in their lives they want to hide and not be accountable for.

> *Take heed to yourself and to the doctrine. Continue in them, for in doing this you will save both yourself and those who hear you* (**1Tim 4:16**).

> *And let us consider one another in order to stir up love and good works, not forsaking the assembly of ourselves together, as is the manner of some* (**Heb 10:25**).

He empowers you to do right

The Greek word for *power (dunamis)* can be translated *"ability."* The Spirit who indwells gives you the ability to carry out the Word of God in your life daily. In every aspect of your life, with your wife, your children, the people at work, with everyone within your sphere of influence, He gives you the power to exemplify the transformed life. Steve was amazed at this. He felt powerless and he was right, in the flesh. But as a Christian he had the power/ability to carry out the principles God had laid out in the scriptures in dealing with his wife in a way that would glorify God. This is why it is so critical for all believers, through the Spirit, to study and practice the Word in their lives daily and be faithful to a local church where the Bible is accurately taught and where each believer can minister to others by their Spiritual gifts. Your life should be known as *"other oriented,"* not self-oriented. This selfish kind of thinking is what got you into trouble to begin with and always will. Letting go of self and being focused on others will truly bring freedom and clarity to your life.

But you will receive power [ability] when the Holy Spirit has come upon you; and you shall be witnesses to Me in Jerusalem, and in all Judea and Samaria, and to the end of the Earth (Acts 1:8; see also Mic 3:8).

He sets you apart (sanctification) for a holy purpose

This *setting apart* has to do with your election by God before the foundation of the world *and* your progressive sanctification through the indwelling Spirit. The Spirit sets you apart for a holy purpose. An understanding of this is critical to your daily life. As you have already read in our study, God Himself has chosen you to be set apart from the world system and to be wholly-owned by Him in your thoughts, motives, and relationships. Just as the holy vessels of the Temple in Jerusalem were set apart for a special and holy purpose, so you have been set apart by the Holy Spirit unto Christ to live a righteous life. You are to be a slave of righteousness and not a slave to sin. This again gives direction as to choices you make. Are they worthy of your high and holy calling? Does watching pornography, using drugs, using foul language, getting anger, gossiping, or any other choice of sin fall in line with your holy calling?

> *Because God from the beginning [before time began] chose you for salvation through sanctification by the means of the Spirit and belief in the truth (Word)* (**2 Thess 2:13**).

> *Elect [Called-out ones] according to the foreknowledge of God the Father, in sanctification of the Spirit, for the purpose of obedience* (**1Pet 1:2**).

Before time began God elected you. The word in Greek for "elects" means *'to pick out from among many."* The whole human race has been condemned by the Lord due to sin against Him. It takes only one sin to separate from the Lord. But out of the whole condemned human race God has chosen some to be part of that redeemed gift He has promised to His Son (see John 6:37,40; 17:24; 1 Cor. 15:28; Titus 1:2). These texts also show that God had "foreknowledge" about those being elected. The Greek word means "a predetermined relationship in the knowledge of God." It does not refer to an awareness of what is going to happen in the future, as though God looked down the corridor of time and saw what decision each human would make, whether they would accept or reject His plan of redemption through Christ. God brought the salvation relationship into His predetermined plan by decreeing it so. This same Greek word is used in 1 Peter 1:20 and is translated "foreordained." You were foreordained, before time began, for salvation, the same way Christ was foreordained to be the sacrifice for your sins (Acts 2:23). The Spirit came and indwelt you at conversion and made complete God's election and plan, until you set foot on the new earth (Rev. 21). You are sanctified by the Spirit which means you are set apart for God's holy work in your life. He makes you more and more Christ-like and sets you apart to minister to others, using your time and gifts for the glory of God. And you are also to be obedient to God's Word (Eph. 2:10). Therefore, glorifying God in your life now is a precursor to what you will be doing fully in eternity. Before Mike and Steve realized this setting apart, they both reacted to their wives both actively in anger, abusive speech, lies and passively by not keeping their word, being quiet and not pleasing the Lord. Their sins mounted and mounted while their troubles continued. It was as though they were digging their own graves of disaster. But once they realized God had set them apart for holy purposes, this changed everything for them. They no longer saw themselves as a victim of their wives or as an enemy. Instead they could be active in growing spiritually and seeing their wives as one's to love as Christ loves them and as a ministry of restoration. Eventually this became the aim of these two men, even if their wives choose a different path in life, they could still please Christ. They would not be considered a failure, and at the same time they could not take personal responsibility for their wives sinful choices. But what they could do is please God in all they do in their lives and marriages.

He comforts you.

Throughout your life, even as a believer, you will face all kinds of trials and hardships. Like in Steve's or Mike's situation or maybe your own difficult situation. Some things in life can not be taught us because of our sinful choices; they have to be learned through the hardships of life. It is in these times that our most precious and lasting lessons are learned toward spiritual growth. Sometimes you may even run about as though God isn't there to help. You act on your own power and strength, making decisions and acting sinfully because you are walking in the flesh and not in the Spirit. In these difficult times you must realize that the Spirit is there to guide and comfort you through the Word He inspired, giving you a special kind of peace only believers can experience. The Spirit will use the Word of God in guiding you daily through each difficult situation. As you are confronted with a particular problem with your wife, you can go to the Word of God, learning how He wants you to react. The Spirit empowers you to both understand the Scriptures and actually carry them out, no matter how difficult it may seem. You should know practically that God is in total control of every situation in your life and that all things will work together for good, even during the difficult times. The Biblical perspective on affliction may help give you tremendous hope in difficult situations, like the one you have been going through.

Blessed be the God and Father of our Lord Jesus Christ, the Father of mercies and God of all comfort, who comforts us in all our tribulations, that we may be able to comfort those who are in any trouble, with the comfort with which we ourselves are comforted by God (**2 Cor 1:3-4; see also John 14:16-26**).

Let's take a quick look at what the Bible has to say about affliction and how we are to view trouble and hard times from God's perspective. Hopefully this will encourage you as it has me.

Affliction and the Spirit's Work.

Biblically, affliction in your life could possibly be due to two reasons, either because of personal sins or perhaps to stretch you to be more Christ-like through trials (this one is not a sin issue).

Consider it all joy when you fall into various trials, knowing that the testing of your faith produces patience. But let patience have its mature work, that you may be mature and complete, lacking nothing (**James 1:2-4**).

Let's use an example here to help you understand. You may have a situation in which trials come your way, not because of sin on your part but to test your faith. James, the half-brother of Jesus, says that you are to make a conscious commitment to face hard times with joy. Joy is not related to your circumstances or feelings, but instead to the unchanging and sovereign reign of God over all events in your life. Nothing catches Him by surprise. And this joy is not necessarily a smile on your face; it is an inner contentment in trusting God. The natural way to respond in the flesh/sin is not to rejoice, but to cast aside the Biblical view in favor of anger, despair, and maybe even resentment toward God. As we will see later, there is affliction caused as a result of your sin, but it must be emphasized here that not all affliction is due to sin.

Throughout church history millions of Christians have suffered and died because of their faith and doctrine. Affliction awaits all believers due to their loving faith toward God and the world's hatred of that. Jesus said that these kinds of afflictions would come. The situation you now find yourself in probably does include repercussions due to your sinful reactions to your wife. But if you walk in the Spirit, in your obedience to God's Word, you may still be the backboard of many abuses by your wife.

And ye shall be hated of all men for my name's sake: but he that endureth to the end shall be saved (**Matt 10:22**).

Then shall they deliver you up to be afflicted, and shall kill you: and ye shall be hated of all nations for my name's sake (**Matt 24:9**).

And ye shall be hated of all men for my name's sake: but he that shall endure unto the end, the same shall be saved (**Mark 13:13**).

But his citizens hated him, and sent a message after Him, saying, we will not have this man to reign over us (**Luke 19:14**).

and ye shall be hated of all men for my name's sake (**Luke 21:17**).

If the world hate you, ye know that it hated me before it hated you **(John 15:18).**

Some additional Scriptures may help you understand why trouble arises in your life.

Let's take a look at a few of these.

a. *The ultimate reason for affliction. The main reason for affliction is not sin, even though that could be a secondary reason. The primary reason is because God's holy name has been shamed.* The term *name* in Scripture reflected one's nature or lifestyle. In our culture the term is used mainly as a label. Not so with names in Bible times. Because the name of God reflects His nature and ways, to mock, shame or reject who and what God is can bring affliction. Israel's witness to the other nations about God was so bad that God brought affliction on them. When you choose to walk in sin or react sinfully to your wife, you as a Christian are ultimately rejecting God's ways and principles.

Then you will know that I am the Lord when I have dealt with you for My Name's sake, not according to your evil ways or according to your corrupt deeds, O Israel, declares the Lord **(Ezek 20:44).**

Thus says the Lord God, 'It is not for your sake, O house of Israel that I am about to act, but for My Holy Name, which you have profaned among the nations where you went. I will vindicate the holiness of my great Name which has been profaned among the nations, which you have profaned in their midst **(Ezek 36:22).**

b. *God is faithful to afflict.* He never misses any human event in history and isn't blind to the actions of man, but He will be faithful to afflict. However, we must realize that God's children will never suffer the wrath of God. That is reserved for the unsaved, those who's father is of the devil (John 8:44). You, however, may face the discipline of the Lord because He is your loving Father and desires that you move toward Christ-likeness. The Spirit also strives for this very thing in you (1 Cor. 11:32). Your discipline will fall into two basic categories:

1. *Discipline due to habitual sins.* You know these sins are wrong but you refuse to let go of them because of pleasure or escape.

   To him who knows the right thing to do and doesn't do it, to him it is sin (James 4:17).

2. *Discipline for training in Christ-likeness,* called trials, which is not discipline due to sin. Again, as a loving Father, God brings trials into your life to stretch and grow you in the areas that need changing. Even in the turmoil of your marriage, God is at work, stretching you to react in a biblical way.

c. *God is the ultimate mover in all afflictions.* This might be difficult to grasp or accept, but all afflictions ultimately come from our totally sovereign God who controls the entire universe and all events.

> *That man may know from the rising to the setting of the sun that there is no one besides me. I Am the Lord, there is no other, the one forming light and creating darkness, causing peace (well-being) and creating calamity. I am the Lord who does all these things* (**Isa 45:6-7**).

You may be asking, "You mean God is in the midst of my situation?" Yes! He is orchestrating it all too eventually bring glory to Himself and good to you. It may seem difficult now, but He wants to see you through this, stretching you to be Christ-like, acting and thinking like Jesus.

d. *God uses affliction to bring people back to Him.* That is His goal for you. God comes to you first with His Word and permanently indwelling Holy Spirit, by which He helps you to overcome any sin in your life. This is God's first action for His elect. But you may, at times, refuse to change and deal with your habitual sins, so God has to use affliction to generate a "wake-up" call in your life, which hopefully will cause you to have lasting repentance. He may bring affliction in stages, even to the point of death, to save you from destroying yourself further or hurting others.

For this reason many are weak and sick among us and many sleep [are dead] (1 Cor 11:30).

Deliver such a one to Satan for the destruction of his flesh, that his spirit may be saved in the day of the Lord Jesus (1 Cor 5:5).

e. *God's Word brings healing to the afflicted.* During times of affliction, believers will find true peace and solace in God's Word. It brings guidance and direction, correcting our perspective on issues. As you delve into His Word, it helps you soar above your difficult situation and see things the way God does.

He sent His word and healed them and delivered them from their destructions (Psa 107:20).

The Spirit gives you inner joy

This joy that God gives you is not necessarily a smile or happiness; it is an inner joy, known only by believers that God is in total control of their lives. The Spirit Himself will give you this assurance.

For the kingdom of God is not eating and drinking, but righteousness and peace and joy within the sphere of the spirit (Rom 14:17).

The Spirit is not only your intercessor between you and the Lord Jesus, who is your advocate and lawyer, both in prayer and empowerment. The Spirit is also the One who somehow assures your hearts that God is with you, and through that assurance. He gives you this unique inner joy that only a Christian can have. During times of hardship you truly can have a supernatural joy that the world cannot know or understand.

And the peace of God, which surpasses all comprehension, will guard your hearts and minds in Christ Jesus (**Phil 4:7**).

But this joy can be yours only if you choose to be obedient in doing things God's way, even during hard times. When you wife is walking in continual sin, you can react in such a way that pleases God and brings inner peace with God, even though maybe not with your wife. Steve had no joy before this time. Life consisted of what he thought was good days, like being away from his wife. But after a time of biblical counseling and living for the Lord, real joy and peace was found in doing God's will with his wife and kids. Not running away but staying and influencing, no matter what his wife said.

He gives you life fruit

Life fruit is the outward result of the inward work of the Spirit in your life as you daily obey God's Word. The Spirit brings about this fruit in your thinking, your desires, and in your daily walk. Because you are no longer a slave to sin but of righteousness, this change in nature should result in a change in lifestyle and outlook. You will exhibit fruit such as love, joy, peace, patience, kindness, goodness and self-control, even in the midst of a hard situation. Your old ways will diminish as you practice the Word of God in your life daily. This is where you need to practice the Ephesians 4 put-off/put-on principle. [6] Overall, you will exhibit one of either two kinds of fruit in your life: either the fruit of walking in the flesh, which is turmoil, confusion, division, and anger; [7] or the fruit of the Spirit's work in your daily walk.

> *But the fruit of the Spirit is love, joy, peace, longsuffering, kindness, goodness, faithfulness, gentleness, self-control* **(Gal 5:22).**

Mike and Steve were in rough situations, having wives that are difficult to live with is a life struggle no doubt. At first, both thought that no good fruit could come from this. Not so. Diamonds are not made till they are put under great pressure. So many times our greatest spiritual growth occurs under the heat of life's struggles. For it is here that real faith in God and His word are put to the test in our lives and situations. Both men, as they started to practice love, patience, understanding and the dying of selfish desires could understand and have life fruit amongst a difficult marriage. For Mike it proved to be a bulwark of strength. For Steve it was the opening up of his own realization that one of the reasons he remained in a difficult situations was the truth that he actually wanted out of the marriage, wanted to be single again so in his hearts of hearts did things to make his wife miserable and hoping she would leave him. That realization opened up and showed Steve the real ugliness of

---

[6] See Jay Adams, The Christian Counselor's Manual, Pp. 176-216. We will look at this in more detail later in the book.

[7] See Appendix 1 for the self test to see if you're really a Christian or not.

his sins. This is common. One of the problems most people have is the inability to be really honest about their motives for doing things. We spend our life masking them in order to relieve ourselves of guilt and shame till we come to the point that we actually believe we are the ones in the clear when in reality our guilt runs as deep as the oceans in sin. When these reactions hit these two men, it was as though the window was opened to a light in their lives. For the first times they could actually have the ability to look into their motives and take a stark reality check, letting the Spirit do His work of true sanctification through His word. Exchanging greed for expecting nothing. Changing anger for love and most of all, a willingness to make sacrifices for the good of others, as their Lord did. When a seed dies it will bring forth fruit. If it had the ability to choose not to, it would remain alone, unfruitful. But if it dies it will bear much fruit. So it is with us. If we expect nothing, want nothing of our own and desire to do God's will in all our lives, your life will bear much fruit, more than you could ever expect. And when you get older and look back, you will see a road filled with many lives you have touched and blessed in God's love, word and spirit.

He helps you worship God

This is where you now have the ability and access to truly worship God. Unlike any of the other religions in the world, only the born-again Christian, one who has put his faith in Christ, can rightly worship God and have that worship accepted by Him. Jesus made this very clear to the apostles and believers throughout history.

*The true **worshippers** will worship the Father in **Spirit and truth**; for the Father is seeking such to worship Him* (John 4:23-24).

This verse is discussing the human spirit that has been regenerated by the Holy Spirit at conversion. This worship avenue, created purely by the grace of God, gives you access to the throne of God. It must also be mentioned that many around the world "worship" God or some other form of a god. Yet God has made a righteous path to Himself through Christ, the only Messiah. The road to hell is probably marked, "the religious way" yet it leads to destruction.

These people draw near to me with their mouth, and honor me with their lips, but their heart is far from Me. And in vain they worship Me, teaching as doctrines the commandments of men **(Matt 15:8-9).**

Jesus was quoting Isaiah 29:13. Through all of human history people have always been motivated to create their own way to God. It started in Genesis 11 with the tower of Babel, continued in the land of Israel among the delivered people of God, Jesus confronted it again during His ministry on earth, and it is still prevalent today. Many proclaim on television, radio, books, the internet, and even in pulpits that all roads lead to God. This Biblically is a lie from Satan himself.

Jesus said unto him, I am the way, the truth, and the life: no man comes unto the Father, but by me **(John 14:6).**

For anyone to truly worship God, they must accept fully His way to Himself, which is faith toward Christ, repentance of sin, a desire to be obedient to God's Word, and a *willingness* to suffer hardship for doing what's right. For you to both desire and worship God daily is to be walking in obedience to His Word, applying His principles to your difficult situations. Be consecrated in your heart and mind to remain steadfast in following the Lord, no matter how you feel or what your present circumstances are.

He gives you the right and ability to pray

Many people pray in the world, in many different religions, but only those who are truly born-again have the genuine right and the ability to pray and have those prayers heard and acted upon by God. The arena and circumstances in which that occurs is tremendous. The Father in heaven is enthroned. Your Advocate, Christ, (who is your divine Lawyer (1 John 2:1; Heb. 4:14-16), is sitting at the right hand of the Father pleading your prayers before Him. And the Spirit, who is your Intercessor, pleads your prayers before Christ. In this divine process, your prayers are brought before Him where they are acted upon-either yes, no, or wait. This understanding is critical to true spiritual growth in your life.[8] Prayer should be an uncompromised time with the Lord daily.

Praying always with all prayer and supplication in the sphere of the Spirit (Eph 6:18).

---

[8] See Dick Eastman, "The hour that changes the world" (Grand Rapids, Baker Book House, 1978).

> *Likewise the Spirit also helps us in our weakness. For we do not know what we should pray as we should, but the Spirit Himself makes intercession for us* (**Rom 8:26-27**).

In the midst of your situation, prayer is one of the key elements that keeps you close to God and helps you respond to your wife Biblically. In fact, prayer is the thermostat of your daily walk in the Lord. Many times men I have known have actually found a true peace amidst turmoil, all because their focus was right, Prayer, devotion to the Lord and His Word, and a thankful heart, encompassed them, bringing a calm and peaceful heart. Other men I have known quickly drifted from these things and life's situations became difficult, painful and they became engulfed in the turmoil's of life. An interesting side note is about Job. The book of Job teaches us that Job was a righteous man who suffered much through affliction brought on by God, using Satan as one of his tools. It says that Job prayed for his children everyday. That is great, but no where does it say he prayed for his wife. He may have, but it is interesting that it doesn't say that. And it was his wife who apparently nagged at him and probably kept him quite humble and dependant on God. She is the same one who told him, during his severe affliction, to curse God and die-not so good advice. Are you praying daily for your wife in this bad situation? God wants you too.

He always directs you to Christ

The role of the Spirit within the Trinity appears to be one in which He doesn't bring attention to Himself. In Scripture, He brings attention to Christ and Christ alone. This is His direction within your life as well. Not to make you "Spirit-like", but Christ-like. Yet, many segments within the church go directly against the Scriptures, teaching and making the Spirit the focal point in their worship and prayers, and seeking to be "filled" by Him daily. However, nowhere in Scripture are we commanded to seek or pray to the Spirit. His goal is Christ-likeness in the saints; His ministry is sanctification in the saints; His role as God is to keep you God's child through all eternity.[9] It should also be noted here that the Spirit should not be ignored. But since Scriptures themselves show us the pattern and role of the Spirit, believers also should follow that pattern and not add any contradictory teachings. Hence, the Spirit desires for you to react within your difficult situation according to Christ's will. The problem is that you may keep choosing sinful reactions in your situation, all of which keeps compounding the problem and making things worse.

But the helper, the Holy Spirit, whom the Father will send in my name, He will teach you all that I said to you…For he will not speak on His own initiative, but whatever He hears, He will speak **(John 16:13;see also John 14:2; 15:26).**

He uses the Spirit-inspired Scriptures to bring about change in your life

And do not be conformed to this world, but be transformed by the renewing of your mind, that you may prove what is that good and acceptable and perfect will of God **(Rom 12:2).**

---

[9] See my book first book on the Holy Spirit.

It was here that Steve had a big problem. Even though he was a Christian and attended church, his life reflected little fruit. He was like many who lived a semi-religious life but in reality they lived as a worldly person would live. All their decisions, finances and relationships were done as any lost person would do them, usually with selfish reasons attached. It wasn't until Steve was confronted with this that his life began to change. It was here Steve realized the importance of the scriptures and its actual application of it in one's life. The Bible is God breathed, inspired by the Spirit, and He uses it in guiding people. As you study and read this Book, it is through the Spirit that you will experience true and lasting change. *True spirituality does not primarily consist in what you do not do; it is rather in what you do. It is not primarily suppression (what you don't do); it is the expression of living the Word of God through the Spirit's power.* Real spirituality is showing forth a transformed life. It is the work of the Spirit to carry out this purpose through illumination, inspiration, and empowerment to apply the Word in your life daily and in all your difficult situations with your wife.

And take the helmet of salvation and the sword of the Spirit, which is the Word of God (Eph 6:17).

All Scripture is God breathed, and is profitable for doctrine, for reproof, for correction, for instruction, that the man of God may be complete (2 Tim 3:15-16).

Having the presence of the Spirit in your life means you are born-again, saved

If you care about your relationship to God, the sin that is troubling you, your lack of prayer, you might be surprised to hear that those very concerns could be signs that you are saved. For truly any unsaved person will care nothing about these issues. But the truly born-again person will have the desire to please God and surrender to Him any area of his life that would hinder his growth into Christlikeness. You must realize that you are dead to selfish desires and alive to Christ, responding with a servant's attitude, even ministering to your wife who needs help. After all, by God's will, you have been chosen to help effect change in her life. It is no mistake. God the Spirit will empower you to the task, if you choose to intently choose His ways and not your own sinful ways.

For as many as are led by the Spirit, these are the Sons of God (Rom 8:14).

So God, who knows the heart, acknowledged them by giving them the Holy Spirit, just as He did to us (Acts 15:8).

When Mike came for help he thought he had been religious at times in his life but due to all the failures in his marriage he thought it was all his fault and took most of the blame for his wife's reactions. In reality what we found was there were some things in his life that he did wrong, the big one being was his sinking into passivity, both in his marriage and his spiritual walk. He even took on a victim mentality, wanting people to both justify his sinful responses and to gain sympathy from others, something most common among people in this kind of situation. What Mike lacked was a change in his perspective on being accountable to God and responsible to his calling. When you look at the Spirit's work in a believer's life it's inspiring to know He is working in your life as well.

The Spirit's work in the church age and how it all fits together

1) Election (God's choice of people to be saved)
2) Predestination
3) The gospel call (proclaiming he message)
4) The inward call
5) Regeneration (being born again)
6) Conversion (faith & repentance)
7) Justification (right legal standing)   *This happens*
8) Adoption (membership into God's family) *in an instant*
9) Sanctification (right conduct in life): Process
10) Perseverance (remaining in Christ)
11) Death (going to heaven)
12) Glorification (receiving a new, resurrected body)
13) Living forever on the new earth

He testifies to your human spirit that you belong to God

He does this through the Word of God, evidencing to your heart and mind that you have been adopted into the family of God (Rom 8:16).

Who also has sealed us and given us the Spirit in our Hearts as a guarantee **(2 Cor 1:22).**

Now we have received, not the spirit of the world, but the Spirit who is from God, that we might know the things that have been freely given to us by God (1 Cor 2:12).

For to be fleshly minded is death, but to be spiritually minded is life and peace...The Spirit Himself bears witness with our human spirit that we are children of God (**Rom 8:16**).

How is this done? It is by the Spirit producing in you the appropriate effects of His influence. It is His to regenerate the heart and nature, to produce "love, joy, peace, long-suffering, gentleness, goodness, faith, meekness, temperance" (Gal. 5:22, 23). If you have these fruits, then you have evidence of the witnessing of the Spirit within your spirit. If you don't see these things in your life, it could be you are just religious but not saved. You should not necessarily base your salvation on an event or a decision made years ago, this could lead someone into a false sense of security with little evidence of regeneration, sanctification, or desire to be Christ-like. The way to ascertain whether you have the witnessing of the Spirit is by doing an honest and prayerful self-examination to see if these fruits of the Spirit actually exist in your life. If they do not, all your religious activities are in vain. If they are present, these fruits of the Spirit should produce a calm, peaceful and contented frame of mind, even in the midst of turmoil.

Not everyone who says to Me, 'Lord, Lord' shall enter the Kingdom of heaven, but he who does the will of my Father in heaven. Many will say to Me in that day, Lord, Lord, have we not prophesied in your name, cast out demons in your name, and done many wonders in your name? And then I will declare to them, 'I never knew you; depart from Me you who practice lawlessness' (Matt 7:21-23).

What you can do to the Holy Spirit negatively.

You are commanded to walk in the Spirit. That means you choose to be obedient to the Word through the power/ability of the Spirit indwelling you. As a result there will be growth toward Christ-like-ness, blessing and a fellowship with God that brings true peace and joy. But at times you may choose to respond to the Holy Spirit in ways that hinder His work and cause affliction, lack of growth, and a fellowship with God that may seem distant. During such times you chose to sin against your wife by anger, greed over money, selfish-ness or some other fleshly desire. Let's look at a few of those things you may do to the Holy Spirit:

a. **Resisting the Spirit.** This mainly applies to the unsaved and those who may act religious. But the saved at times, to a lesser degree, can fall into this category. How? By your daily decisions to resist the Spirit and walk in sin toward your wife.

   You stiff-necked and uncircumcised in heart and ears! You always resist the Holy Spirit as your fathers did, so do you (Acts 7:51).

   People in this category resist the Holy Spirit's work from without. He ministers to believers using events in life or other

114

believers. Some people may even hear the Word preached or receive it from a Christian witness, but still never make true commitment to Christ and His Word. They continue to resist because **the things of this life have been deemed more of value than the Lord.** The saved, too, can resist the Holy Spirit's continual promptings toward Christ-likeness in all their thoughts, motives, and actions.

You can resist the Spirit by hanging on to habitual sins, being unloving and uncaring toward your wife, children, or other Christian brothers and sisters. Repentance and a sincere desire to please the Lord is required to stop resisting the Spirit. If you fail to do this, the Spirit may bring affliction into your life until repentance is secured.

b. **Grieving the Spirit.** This is used for Christians as stated in Ephesians 4:30:

Do not grieve the Holy Spirit of God, by whom you were sealed for the day of redemption.

"Grieve" means *"to make sorrowful."* The context of this verse is discussing corrupt speech. In Isaiah 63:10, the Hebrews resisted the Spirit, continually forsaking Him and His Word. In spite of God's loving care and provision for them, they continued to rebel against Him (see also Psa. 78:40). The verb used in Isaiah 63:10 for *"resist"* means *"to cause acute pain."* You can grieve the Spirit when you willingly chose sin over righteousness in your life. When your wife is being difficult, when situations in the home are

tough, this is the very time you need to use great discernment in intently choosing to do things God's way. You need to apply God's principles to each and every situation, speaking gracious words of help. God knows the right way to go; the best path is always His choice for you, but when you choose sin instead, He is grieved or made sorrowful. When you are in a hot argument with your wife and you know the right thing to do and choose instead to use anger, revenge or some other sinful reaction, you are grieving the Spirit within you. This potential for sin should be at the front of your mind in each and every situation. Also, this verse provides additional evidence that the Spirit is a divine person, because a mere force or power cannot be grieved.

c. **Quenching the Spirit**. "Quench" is used only once and of Christians.

Do not quench the Spirit **(1 Thess 5:19).**

This verse is another proof that the Spirit is God. It conveys the idea of quenching or putting out a fire. You can quench Him by knowing the right thing to do in your situation but choosing not to do it. Also, when you force your way into situations, relationships, or ministries without any prayerful consideration or consulting the Word, you are quenching the Spirit. Every time you sinfully react to your wife, even when she is walking in sin, you are quenching the Spirit, dousing intently His work in your life.

Therefore, to him who knows the right thing to do and does not do it, to him it is sin **(James 4:17).**

d. **Tempting the Spirit.** The word *"tempt"* in Acts 5:9 means *"to try or test."* It comes from the Greek *peirazo* and has a twofold meaning: to try, or to put to the test. God will test men (Heb. 11:17); men test God at times in their lives (Acts 15:10; 5:9); men test themselves (2 Cor. 13:5); and men test other men. In Acts 5:9, Peter tells Ananias that he not only lied to the Holy Spirit, but that he put the Spirit to the test, to deceive those in the early church. Can Christians today test the Holy Spirit? Yes! You can test Him when you distrust His guidance or choices, and when you think you can get away with sin done "secretly," not realizing the Spirit sees all because He indwells you. In reality there is no such thing as a "secret sin" with God. It is a foolish idea if you think you can sin and either get away with it or keeps it hidden. You, as a believer, should never test God this way. God does react to every sinful action you take. But what's missing about this point many times is that you hurt yourself by how you choose to react sinfully to difficult situations in your home. Those choices cause you to corrupt your temple, defiling it in ways that bring shame to God's name and His purpose, and maybe even causing others to sin. This point needs to be taken very seriously because God takes it very seriously. If you don't, God will orchestrate things in your life until you do. *It's your choice; the best way or the hard way.*

e. **Defiling the temple of the Spirit.** A temple generally means the dwelling place of a deity. In the Scriptures, this phrase "temple of the Spirit" is used two ways: first, in 1 Corinthians 3:16-17 of the Spirit indwelling the body of Christ; second, in 1 Corinthians 6:19 of the Spirit indwelling the individual believer. There are people who will try to hurt or injure the temple, both corporately (6:19) and individually (3:16). Some would be the cults, occults, or Satan himself. Besides these things, when you choose to act sinfully toward your wife you are defiling your temple. You are either a defiled temple because of your choice to sin, or you are a clean temple because you choose to walk in the Spirit, in obedience to God's Word, living a life of daily repentance.

Overview of The Spirits Ministry To Believers.
(How He impacts your daily life)

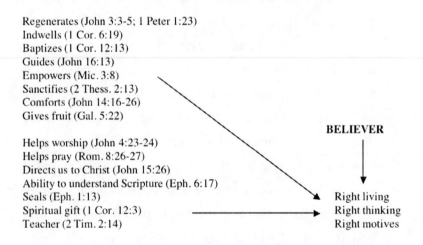

Regenerates (John 3:3-5; 1 Peter 1:23)
Indwells (1 Cor. 6:19)
Baptizes (1 Cor. 12:13)
Guides (John 16:13)
Empowers (Mic. 3:8)
Sanctifies (2 Thess. 2:13)
Comforts (John 14:16-26)
Gives fruit (Gal. 5:22)

Helps worship (John 4:23-24)
Helps pray (Rom. 8:26-27)
Directs us to Christ (John 15:26)
Ability to understand Scripture (Eph. 6:17)
Seals (Eph. 1:13)
Spiritual gift (1 Cor. 12:3)
Teacher (2 Tim. 2:14)

BELIEVER

Right living
Right thinking
Right motives

You and your Spiritual Gifts

At your conversion, you were given the Spirit to indwell you for several reasons: empowerment to carry out the Word of God, the ability/power to overcome any sin, manifestation of spiritual fruit in your life, prayer, worship and the desire and ability to serve others in the body of Christ. His presence is a sign you are saved and His pledge that you will make it to eternity. Also at conversion the Spirit gives you spiritual gifts that you could not otherwise exercise. It is"giftedness" from God by grace. A spiritual gift cannot be earned, pursued, or worked at (Acts 8:18-24). It is the divine will and choice of the Spirit to perfectly give each believer a gift that is specially crafted not only to fit them, but to benefit the Body of Christ.

But one and the same Spirit works all these things, distributing to each one individually as He wills **(1 Cor 12:11)**.

Gifts are not to be used pridefully, but humbly, realizing they are of God the Spirit who ministers through you in helping others in the body of Christ, the church.

You are to be good stewards of these gifts. A steward is responsible for another's resources. Since you were given a spiritual gift at conversion, it is a terrible thing not to use it in serving others. The Spirit has designed the body to fit together in such a way as to manage and help each other. The lack of a gift's use leaves a gap, a sort of missing piece in the body of Christ, the church.

Jesus talked about this in Matthew 25:15.

For the Kingdom of heaven is like a man traveling to a far country, who called his own servants and delivered his goods to them. And to one he gave five talents, to another two, and to another one, to each according to his own ability, and immediately he went on a journey.

Along with the above verse, compare Matthew 21:33, where the same type of departure is ascribed to God after He sets up the ancient economy. In both cases, God leaves all those spiritual ministries to men so they might graciously minister in the church to each other. The Spirit divinely chose to give gifts to believers, according to the ability of each one (see Rom 12:6; 1 Cor 12:4; Eph 4:11). God gives you gift(s) which He expects you to fulfill and use. So He makes distinctions among people in regard to abilities and in the powers and opportunities of usefulness; requiring simply that they occupy those ministries and discharge their duties appropriately (1Cor 4:7).

There are several things about spiritual gifts that you must understand.

a. **Every Christian has a spiritual gift.** There is no such concept in Scripture of an ungifted believer. But most do not know or use their gift as the Spirit would want them to.[10] Do you know your spiritual gift? Are you being a wise steward and using it to serve others? Jesus one day is going to talk to you about this very thing.

Do not neglect the gift that is in you (**1 Tim 4:14**).

---

[10] See also Romans 12:4-8; 1 Corinthians 12:4-12; 1 Peter 4:10-11.

As each one has received a gift, minister it to one another as good stewards of the manifold grace of God **(1 Pet 4:10).**

But the manifestation of the Spirit is given to each one for the profit of all **(1 Cor 12:7).**

b. **True fulfillment and joy in the Lord comes from exercising one's giftedness in the local church body.**

Only as you use your God given gifts in the church will you find true contentment, fulfillment and usefulness with your spiritual family. That is the way God designed it and the neglect of it could lead to spiritual apathy and little true spiritual growth.

For it is God who works in you both to will and to do for His Good pleasure **(Phil 2:13).**

c. **Each gift is designed by the Spirit to perfect the body of Christ.**

And He [Spirit] Himself gave some to be apostles, some prophets, some evangelists and some pastor/teachers for the equipping of the saints for the work of the ministry, for the edifying of the body of Christ **(Eph 4:11-12).**

The Trinity desires for you to know and use your spiritual gifts effectively and to the glory of God. Paul the apostle wrote that the believer's in the Galatian churches were so blessed to have the promises of the Spirit, and yet they became so apathetic about it. God wants you to understand how important gifts are. For the one who considers himself a Christian and yet cares little about the exercise of his perfectly chosen and designed spiritual gift is like a man hired to be a C.E.O. of a powerful and influential company but instead is found fishing at the local pond.

Are you so foolish? Having begun in the Spirit, are you now being made perfect by the flesh? **(Gal 3:3).**

d. **No one member's gift is more important than another's.** All believers were given a special gift (s) according to what the Spirit decided for the betterment of the Body and the will of God (1 Cor 12:12- 24). Believers need each other in the body of Christ for mutual growth, ministry, and encouragement, all through the Spirit in obedience to the Word of God.

But now there are many members yet one body and those members of the body which we think to be less honorable, on these we bestow greater honor; and our unpresentable parts have greater modest...but God composed the body [church] having given greater honor to that part which lacks it, that there should be no division in the body, but that the members should have the same care for one another **(1 Cor 12:23-25).**

Some gifts are more prominent than others, especially the speaking gifts. But this is due to their role within the church. Any believer who seeks to use whatever gift the Spirit has given them will be as valuable a servant to Christ as the apostle Paul himself. A gift is not the only issue, but one's faithfulness in using it.

e. **The spiritual gifts are listed in Romans 12:6-8, 1 Corinthians 12:8-10; 12:28; 1 Peter 4:11.** As you study these lists, you should realize that these are not perfect or exhaustive lists. They vary in use and practice. In time, God will make known to you your gift.

f. **How to know your spiritual gift.**
    Since every believer has a spiritual gift, there should be the desire to know it in order to be much more effective and focused. Below are some solid ways to find one's spiritual gift.

    1. Start praying and humbly ask God to guide you to know your spiritual gift. But realize this may take years. Be patient! Realize you are never commanded to seek a gift; the Holy Spirit has already decided which one you have. Be faithful in the little things God gives you, with your family and church.
    2. Do a Bible study on what the spiritual gifts are (see above).
    3. Get involved in a good local church. Try several different ministries there. See where God leads. Be

faithful in serving others. But make sure it is a Bible-teaching church that believes in the full authority and inspiration of the Scriptures. I realize there are many so-called churches to choose from, but many have compromised the Word of God and integrated humanistic philosophy and worldly psychology into their practices. Steer clear of these. Integration of those ideas is dangerous to one's spiritual growth and Biblical ministry to others. As a believer, if you serve others in a church with integrational methods, it is only a disservice to Christ and others. God has given the church Biblical principles that are powerful in helping others in counseling, home life, work, business practices, and every other area of life. The problem is that many "Christians" believe the Scriptures are not sufficient enough for life's concerns. Therefore they believe they must create humanistic reasoning in helping others with spiritual issues. The Bible is clear, it is sufficient for all problems.

All Scripture is given by inspiration of God, and is profitable for doctrine, for reproof, for correction, for instruction in righteousness (2 Tim 3:16)

For this reason we also thank God without ceasing, because when you received the Word of God which you heard from us, you welcomed it not as the word of men, but as it is in truth, the Word of God, which also effectively works in you who believe (**I Thess 2:13**).

4. Ask other mature believers about what they think your gift may be. Sometimes, as others see you faithfully serving over time, can they objectively see things you may not see at first. Ask those who you know, those mature ones.

The Spirit's Example to You of Being 'Other-oriented.'

As noted earlier, the Spirit's role is to point you to Christ, giving you the ability to overcome sinful practices and grow in Christ-likeness in all areas of your life, including responding rightly to your wife. One of those major areas is the change from being self-oriented to other-oriented. It is here that the battle over sin often hinges. Before coming to Christ, your whole life was self-centered, as though the world revolved around you. When you were born again, you died to selfish desires of the flesh. Here we will see the Spirit's example within the holy Trinity of how to view your wife as more important than yourself, even when she is being difficult, selfish, and walking in the flesh.

Or do you not know that as many of us as were placed into Christ Jesus were placed into His death? Therefore we were buried with Him through this placing into death, that just as Christ was raised from the dead by the glory of the Father, even so we also should walk in newness of life...The old man was crucified with Him that the body of sin might be done away with, that we should no longer be slaves of sin…Having been set free from the slavery of sin, *you have become slaves of righteousness* **(Rom 6:3-4, 6-7,** **18).**[11]

Your spiritual growth and maturity is gauged by your desire to put others first, to walk in a humble way of life rather than pushing others out of the way to get what you want, even in ministry. This failure to put others first is probably what causes many arguments in your home between your wife and you. You both want your own way. That is why James said;

Where do battles and fights come from among you? Do *they not come from your desires for pleasure that war in* *your members? You desire and do not have. You lust and do* *not have…You are envious and cannot obtain; so you fight* *and quarrel. Therefore submit to God, resist the devil and* *he will flee from you. Draw near to God and He will draw* *near to you…Humble yourself in the sight of the Lord, and* *He will lift you up"* **(James 4:1-2; 7-8).**

Be kindly affectionate to one another with brotherly love, *in honor giving preference to one another* **(Rom 12:10).**

As I have ministered over the years and worked with hundreds of people in different capacities, one of the things I've learned, sometimes the hard way through my own selfish desires, is that the believer's goal should be focused on being other-oriented. This is

---

[11] The author has inserted the words "placed into" and "placing into" as translations of the word *baptized.*

very clear, both in Scripture and when I have come across a believer who is truly a humble person, full of love, one who thinks of others as more important than themselves. These kinds of people appear to be rare among so many in the world, because we live in a world in which pride, self-esteem, self-worth, self-goals, self first is pushed everywhere. It seems that everybody is being taught that they are number one and the world must beckon to their needs or desires. But those believers, who realize their position in Christ and the loving grace that was shed upon them, truly have a humble attitude toward all. They stick out as roses among thorns. It should be the believer's goal, as it was Christ's, to live a life of being selfless, humble, and gentle.

He humbled Himself and became obedient to the point of death, even death on the cross **(Phil 2:8).**

Take My yoke upon you and learn from Me, for I am gentle and lowly in heart and you will find rest for your souls **(Matt 11:29).**

In looking at this most important aspect of the Christian's life, the Trinity has given us the supreme example of this other-oriented principle. Each member of the Godhead deserves full worship, honor, and dignity. It is interesting to note that God the Father keeps Himself in the background and puts forth His adorable Son. God the Son keeps Himself in the background and gives the ministry of glorifying Himself to the Holy Spirit and the Father. God the Spirit keeps Himself in the background and manifests the Son.

a) God the Father. Matthew 17:5. The Father uplifts the Son.
b) God the Son. John 17:1, 4, 6. The Son uplifts the Father.
c) God the Spirit. John 14:26; 16:13-14. The Spirit uplifts the Father and the Son.

Jesus sent out the seventy-two to preach the gospel and perform miracles. Upon their return and hearing all their good reports, He rejoiced in the power of the Holy Spirit. Who did He praise and exalt? The Holy Spirit? Himself? Neither one of these. He praised God the Father. The Spirit's influence in His life urged Jesus to praise the Father. Here we have an example of two persons within the Trinity honoring the third; God the Son and God the Spirit praising God the Father.

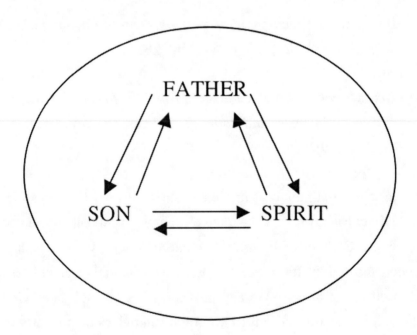

And at that very time He rejoiced greatly in the Holy Spirit and said, 'I praise you, O Father, Lord of Heaven and earth" (Luke 10:21).

This illustration above, of the Divine Trinity, exemplifies for you the other-oriented life you are to have. The Spirit within you gives you the motivation and ability to show forth love and put others before yourself. Practically, this attitude also applies toward your wife. You are to see her as more important than yourself and your own desires. She is one who needs to see a Godly example, one who needs ministry. *This is your calling.* This also goes directly against everything you see and hear in the world. But as a Christian you are to react Biblically, through the power of the Spirit in obedience to His inspired Word. The Scriptures listed below provide principles that all believers should be working towards.

The One-Another Principle	Scripture	Main idea
Prefer	Romans 12:10	Prefer one another in honor
Devoted	Romans 12:10	Be devoted to one another in love
Same mind	Romans 12:16	Have a modest opinion of yourself in relation to one another

Build up	Romans 14:19	Pursue that which makes for peace and building up one another
Accept	Romans 15:7	Accept one another as Christ also accepted you to God's glory
Admonish	Romans 15:14	Full of goodness, knowledge, and able to admonish one another
Sue not	1 Corinthians 6:7	Do not have lawsuits with one another; no one really wins
Care for	1 Corinthians 12:25	Have the same care for one another, which averts division
Envy not	Galatians 5:26	Do not envy one another, but manifest a spirit of contentment
Truthful to	Ephesians 4:25	Speak truthfully in every matter to one another
Kind to	Ephesians 4:32	Be kind, pleasant, and tender-hearted to one another
Subject to	Ephesians 5:21	Be subject to those in authority over you

Regard	Philippians 2:3	Don't be conceited, but regard one another as more important than yourself
Lie not to	Colossians 3:9	Do not lie to one another, since you have put that habit away
Bear with	Colossians 3:13	Bearing with and forgiving one another, as the Lord forgave you
Teach	Colossians 3:16	Teach and admonish one another with the words of God
Love	1 Thessalonians 3:12	May the Lord cause you to increase in love for one another
Comfort	1 Thessalonians 5:11	Therefore comfort each other and edify one another
Encourage	1 Thessalonians 5:11	Encourage one another, especially as to your faith in the Lord
Peace with	1 Thessalonians 5:13	Live in peace and harmony with one another

Seek good for	1 Thessalonians 5:15	Seek after that which is good for one another and all men
Pray for	1 Timothy 2:1	Prayer…made for all men
Stimulate	Hebrews 10:24	Consider ways to stimulate one another to love and good deeds
Speak not against	James 4:11	Do not speak slanderously against one another
Complain not	James 5:9	Don't complain against one another, that you may not be judged
Confess	James 5:16	Confess your sins to one another (to those you have sinned against)
Hospitable to	1 Peter 4:9	Be hospitable to one another, generous and without complaint
Serve	1 Peter 4:10	Use God's gracious gifts to serve one another
Humble toward	1 Peter 5:5	Be humble to one another, knowing God is opposed to pride

Greet	1 Peter 5:14	Greet one another in a caring and loving manner
Fellowship with	1 John 1:7	We have fellowship with one another as we walk with God [12]

Along with practicing these one another's and letting them become a part of your daily walk in the Lord, through the power of the Spirit and in obedience to the Word of God, the Spirit's influence should affect every area of your life (for He encourages you to daily read and practice God's Word, letting it sanctify every area of your life). The problems come when you don't do that.

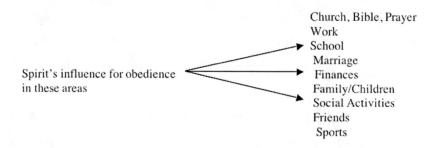

One of the things that so shocked Mike and his bad relationship with his wife was the reality of how he was acting and living. As he received counseling the ugliness of his own sin was shown clearly by the scriptures. He saw how selfish his ways were toward his wife. How he viewed money, cars, homes and love was all based upon selfish desires, not God's love at all. When you have two leaches living together what you end up with is a mad fight to use each

[12] Data from Dr. Stuart Scott; The Masters College, Biblical Counseling course, 2002.

other, and that's where Mike and his wife were. She wanted more and more and he wanted to give little. The fight went on from one argument to another. As Mike though began to grow in his spiritual walk with the Lord did he face his sins and repented. Sometimes a man doesn't see how ugly his sins are until he looks into the mirror of scriptures.

The Spirit's Work in Giving Hope during Times of Affliction, Due to a Bad Marriage.

Now may the God of hope fill you with all joy and peace in believing that you may abound in hope by the power/ability of the Holy Spirit (**Rom 15:13**).

At the writing of this book, the word hope is being announced everywhere, on the television, radio, and the streets. If anything is to be the capstone word in the writing of this period of history, it should be hope.

Because hope is being tossed around everywhere, as a Christian how does your view of hope and how you envision it compare to worldly hope? I realize there is general hope for the world, like there is common grace given by God. Within this context, hope is being used as a capstone to cover despair and loss of life. Without hope, what would people have? As our two friends viewed life (Mike and Steve) there wasn't a lot of hope. Life was filled with despair, disillusionment and no hope. Their wives had so beaten them down verbally and tried to gain control of the relationship that they both came to the point of complete frustration. But it is often true that it takes affliction in one's life to awakened people for the need of God and His ways. This is where Mike and Steve looked to and found hope and direction.

As a Christian, your reaction to problems in your marriage should automatically come with the resounding words of hope. This idea of hope with affliction has always stirred me personally, and that's why I decided to include it in this book. I wanted to teach readers how Christians can have a real hope during any kind of affliction, including that of a marriage which is difficult. The Spirit of God is at work, molding and shaping you into Christ-like decision-making and thinking, urging you, stretching you to react to problems and conflicts in a way that goes directly against your old ways.

When affliction hits members of a godless generation, all they have is a hollow kind of hope to cover over their despair. As a Christian, though, hope not only deals with despair but goes far beyond that and gives an objective reality to look forward to. How does hope apply when affliction hits a Christian? First, we must layout out some basic Biblical principles concerning affliction and how hope is an important ingredient in such times. I'll deal with the practical side of how all this affects your life. There are eight foundational principles concerning the Biblical view of affliction and hope that need to be mentioned first.

The Eight Foundational Pillars About God, Affliction, And Hope.

PILLAR #1
God is a loving, merciful, and compassionate person.

This is a foundational principle we must understand as grounds for a right perspective on life. During times of affliction, we usually hear someone ask, *"Why does God allow such tragedy? Is He so cold and non-caring to allow something like this to happen?"* Or others might think, *"doesn't He see how much anguish I have? Why doesn't He do something about my wife? She is being so mean!"*

When asking these heart felt questions, if we are to have a proper perspective on hope during affliction, we must first understand that God is a very loving and merciful God toward us fallen creatures. And within this affliction He is showing His love.

He sent His word and healed them, and delivered them from their afflictions (Psa 107:20).

This is a great verse of hope for believers, that even during times of afflictions God cares and acts for us (see Psa. 99:9; 103:10-14). He is not a harsh mean God who is looking to make our lives miserable. Neither is He a non-caring, non-enacting God who seems far off. He is acting; He is caring. We can praise and thank Him for His care and concern for us as His children.

Let not the oppressed return dishonored; let the afflicted and needy praise Thy name (Psa 74:21).

Because of this verse our hope can be greatly increased during times of trouble and hardship. We can truly be thankful to God for all things that come our way. Our "spiritual perspective" has been widened. God's very nature is one of mercy, compassion, and care.

God knows our struggles, and pain, and He is close by. The problem is not with God. It is with you and your desires, your sinful reactions, sometimes your selfish motives. These cause a lot of trouble and a skewed perspective on God's sovereignty. A sincere look at your own heart and motives is needed. An honest repentance is needed, and the application of God's Word to your situation is the answer.

PILLAR #2
As a loving Father, God is faithful to afflict us.

And that in faithfulness you have afflicted me (Psa 119:75).

After studying this verse I realized that it gives me great hope. When I first read this, I was taken back by what it said. But because I belong to God, He is a loving Father and in that love He afflicts me due to my own stubborn desires to sin, and thus better conform me to the image of Christ. When I gained this perspective I realized again that God is not far off but near and intimate with all my ways. Nothing takes Him by surprise, and any affliction that comes our way is for our good and His glory. In fact, God is so great that **He uses affliction as a means to show forth His divine attributes of love and mercy to all creation.** Even when your wife is acting in a way that is very wrong, God is somehow, unknown to you, orchestrating everything for your good and His glory. I know this sounds strange, but God is working things according to a bigger perspective than yours.

PILLAR #3
Ultimately God will justify the afflicted.

Ultimately one must realize that God will justify the cause of those who have been afflicted by people who are walking in sinful ways. He will deal out justice to all of those who, throughout the centuries, have tried to strip believers of their hope and purity of faith. Our focus needs to be on God, the author and finisher of our faith and righteous judge who fulfills His task. No single human aggression or sin will go unjudged by Him. All the acts of men will one day be dealt with.

> *I know the Lord will maintain the cause of the afflicted, and bring justice for the poor. Surely the righteous shall give thanks to your name; the upright shall dwell in your presence* (**Psa 140:12-13**).

Isn't that such a great hope! No matter what affliction is occurring either around you or directly in your life, you can know and have hope that God Himself will judge those who afflict and deliver you to His presence (see Psa 146:7-10; Isa 33:1; Prov 3:34;)

God himself will take care of everything according to His perfect justice. Your focus should never be to participate in any of her sinful actions. Instead minister to her, even in the midst of turmoil. Leave discipline and judgment to God's domain. And instead of anger for her have compassion and mercy because she is the one who will eventually suffer more than you ever will.

> *So then, my beloved brethren, let every man be swift to hear, slow to speak, slow to wrath, for the wrath of man does not produce the righteousness of God* (**James 1:19-20**).

PILLAR #4
All believers one day will have deliverance (salvation) from all afflictions.

For the Lord takes pleasure in His people: He will beautify the afflicted with salvation **(Psa 149:4).**

This should be your focus of hope. God cares for you so much that you will be beautified with total deliverance. What a great hope! Deliverance in the Scriptures can be a word used for salvation. Yes, you suffer affliction now due to the fall, but one day affliction will no longer exist in the new earth and eternity. Yes, you may feel hurt, as though God Had abandoned you. But God is very close, knowing all your ways. Your task is to focus on Him whose plan for believers will be accomplished. You are not alone. Don't focus on the events, but on the ultimate goals of God.

PILLAR #5
Affliction wakes you up from Spiritual apathy.

Affliction gives you an awakening from God because it is a divine call to a serious consideration of your personal relationship with Him. As I will discuss later, not all affliction is caused by sin, but all afflictions should draw you closer to God.

Before I was afflicted I went astray, but now I keep your Word **(Psa 119:76; see also 119:71).**

I sometimes wander from my personal relationship with the Lord and He seems to use affliction as a tool to awaken me and get me back on the "highway of holiness" (Isa 35:8). Whenever affliction comes your way, the Spirit within you may be pricking your conscience toward dealing with sin. Careful thought and meditation needs to be exercised at this point. **A key point to remember is that our hearts are more resistant to righteous change. Therefore the affliction will be tailor made to break you and effect the needed change. God always knows best!**

It's been my experience that for most people, it takes affliction in our lives till we are willing to do things God's way. For Steve, he knew the word of God, knew he wasn't being obedient to God yet remained steadfast in his sinful ways toward his wife. It wasn't until God brought affliction, using his wife as one of those many tools at His disposal, that Steve was broken and was now willing to listen to God.

PILLAR # 6
Affliction purifies us to our relationship to God.

Affliction has a purifying effect on a believer's life. Let me share my heart for a moment. We are stubborn people who are bent to sinfully stray from God. I have observed that for me and those I've known, it usually takes affliction and trouble to motivate us towards repentance, a new desire to obey God's Word.

Desire for plenty of money, a good job, worldly fame, or good relationships can easily put God on the sidelines of our affections. We might still be going to church every Sunday, but the first love we had at salvation has grown dim. Then suddenly, out of nowhere, comes affliction. Our comfortable world is now tossed to and fro and we frantically realize within our hearts that we must run to God. When all is lost, when all the things that pushed God from the center of our life have been stripped away, suddenly nothing else matters in this life but our personal relationship to God. Then a new desire for pure obedience to His Word beams into our life like the morning sun through the kitchen window. It's a feeling not sought for before affliction arrives, but one that is refreshing at its coming.

The world may seem different to you when affliction comes. It may appear empty and all the things you once trusted in become so miniscule. Why has this new situation drowned you so? God came to you first with His love, mercy, and Word. Again and again the message came, but your lazy and stubborn spirit pursued pleasurable desires that entice the fallen flesh. Then the Spirit had to use affliction to awaken you to the real spiritual realities of your life. I know this is true because it has happened to me. The things that really matter come to light. Everything else falls behind; many of the past sinful desires fade. Now a new desire to please God and know Him more surrounds your life and brings true peace, comfort, contentment, but most of all Hope. Hope that all chaos will cease and order will once more reign. This time God will be at the helm. This of all pillars is most intimate to me. Why? Because I've experienced this storm and have come through it with lasting impressions.

It is good for me that I have been afflicted, that I may learn your Statutes. The law of your mouth is better to me than thousands of coins of gold and silver (Psa 119:71-72).

David had everything, but it took affliction to purify his life and awaken him to the true values of life (see also Job 36:7-15; 2 Chron. 12:8; 1 Sam. 12:15; 1 Kings 9:3-6).

I'll never forget the words Mike spoke to me once. He said, *"Your know, for a long time I thought I was the wronged. That my wife was the only real problem. But God has shown me that I was also part of the problem and that He held me responsible for my sin and wanted me to change. Now that my eyes have been opened I see much clearer now."*

PILLAR #7,
We all deserve eternal affliction.

We all deserve not only daily but eternal affliction. This foundational truth came to me as I was studying "hope during affliction." During times of affliction, I always saw them as unusual and the timing as the worst. But after this study I realized that my perspective was not Biblical. Now I realize all members of humanity deserve constant, hopeless affliction for their rebellion and sin against God. But God has spread His grace upon all who believe, due to His love and mercy; and He has given us a great hope of eternal salvation. Not that we deserve God's grace, not at all, but by His grace He stooped down to help a sinner like me and pour within my heart a great hope. The hope is that all afflictions in my life will have true and everlasting meaning. I also realized through my study that when affliction comes, it is from my loving Father who disciplines me so I can be conformed to His son's image. It is never as the wrath of One who is far off and doesn't care. He does care for us all very much, and He knows all our ways, hurts, pains, weaknesses and desires. He knows us all intimately.

Lord, You have searched me and known me. You know my sitting down and my rising up; you understand my thoughts afar off. You comprehend my path and my lying down, and are acquainted with all my ways (Psa 139:1-3).

PILLAR # 8
Affliction awaits those who reject the truth.

This is the last foundational truth, which sadly takes away all hope in this life. I listed this foundational truth concerning "hope during affliction" last because it is the ultimate conclusion for one who knows the truth, has tasted of God and His truth and yet rejects it all. This truly is hope lost.

Harsh affliction is for him who forsakes the way, and he who hates correction will die (**Prov 15:10**).

Scriptures contain some startling things to warn those who continue in sin without repentance rather than turn to righteousness.

The way of the unfaithful is hard (**Prov 13:15b**).

For when you were slaves of sin, you were free in regard to righteousness. What fruit did you have then in the things of which you are now ashamed? For the end of those things is death (**Rom 6:20-21**).

Deliver such a one to Satan for the destruction of the flesh, that his [human] spirit may be saved in the day of the Lord Jesus (**1 Cor 5:5**).

For this reason many are weak and sick among you, and many sleep [die] (**1 Cor 11:30**).

If anyone sees his brother sinning, a sin which does not lead to death, he will ask, and He will give him life for those who commit sin not leading to death. There is sin leading to death **(1 John 5:16).**

These verses listed above clearly show that believers who habitually choose to walk in sin and refuse to repent could have their lives taken away so that no further destruction occurs in their lives or the lives of others. God seeks the purity of the church and sends the Spirit to accomplish it. These sins cause the Spirit of God to end the believer's life. It's not one particular sin, but whatever sin is the final one for the tolerance and patience of God (see also Prov 6:12; 15; 16:14; 24:16).

How To respond To Affliction and Have Hope Through The Power of the Spirit and the Word.

Steve had an anger problem and because he was walking in the flesh and responded to his difficult wife in sinful ways, this compounded his problems even more. More greed, anger and revenge filled his mind from day to day, until he couldn't take it no longer, so he moved out, thinking that peace in his life would be found by abandoning his responsibilities. This is never the case, especially for a Christian. It took some time of counseling for Steve to realize what God wanted him to do in how to respond biblically to his wife. It was in this that peace was found for Steve.

As I studied the afore-mentioned Scriptures, I did it all with a view to share my own heart. I've experienced many afflictions and sometimes I responded to them with hope and other times without hope, due to my own sin. Following is a list of ways I've learned to respond rightly to affliction. Applying them has given me a great hope in God and my future.

During affliction, I am to commit my soul to God, trusting Him because He is the God of truth.

Because He speaks truth, I can always trust what He says. He is God, the God who will do all for His glory and my good.

Into your hands I commit my spirit; you have redeemed me, O Lord, the God of truth. I have hated those who regard useless idols: but I trust in the Lord. I will be glad and rejoice in your mercy, for you considered my affliction; you have known my soul in adversities **(Psa 31:5-8).**

It was while studying these verses that something very strange happened to me on a Sunday afternoon at the Grace Seminary library.

After finishing my studies on how to respond to affliction, I gathered up all my books and headed for my truck to get something to eat before church. As I walked out to the parking space, I found that it was empty! My truck had been stolen. My first reaction was dismay. But after a minute, all that I had been studying that afternoon became very real to me. I could truly thank the Lord from my heart for even this event and pray for those people who stole my truck. It was because of God's Word I was able to have hope in affliction. Usually I would have been very upset and angry. But a cool contentment ran over me because I knew God was in complete control and did all for good. Because of this I could be thankful instead of bitter.

Great hope can be mine if during affliction I'm in prayer more often.

My personal prayer life appears to increase when affliction hits, whether the trial is due to sin or not.

In return for my love they are my accusers, but I give myself to prayer: thus they have rewarded me evil for good, and hatred for my love **(Psa 109:4-5).**

I know that prayer can be sweeter during times of affliction and that a well of hope can spring up from my heart. But my desire is that my whole life will have a proper attitude of prayer. Prayer is the nerve that gives you strength during times of turmoil in your home.

Hope is mine when I realize that God is the ultimate mover in all afflictions that comes my way.

You, who have shown me great and severe afflictions, shall revive me again, and bring me up again from the depths of the earth **(Psa 71:20).**

Even during times of great afflictions, I have had deep hope in God because I know that all these things are God-ordained so that my relationship to Him will be better and closer. Knowing that God is in complete control brings me great hope no matter what happens.

This also allows you to see your wife's meanness as an avenue to do right toward her, thus putting to practice Biblical ways rather than your old ways of anger, revenge, or pride.

God will always deliver me from affliction.

We are not immune to affliction, but I know that our loving Father brings affliction into our lives for His glory and for our good. He also may choose not to remove the affliction quickly, but use it for many years to do a work in your life. But ultimately you will be delivered.

God is to us a God of deliverance; and to God the Lord belongs escapes from death (Psa 68:20).

Jerry Bridges summed it all up on this point when he said;

No one can act and no circumstances can occur outside the bounds of God's sovereign will. But this is only one side of His sovereignty.

The other side, which is just as important to our trusting Him, is that no plan of God's can be thwarted. God has an over-arching purpose for all believers: To conform us to the likeness of His Son, Jesus Christ [13]

I have another great hope that even though many afflictions may rise up around me, I will always be lifted up by God through them all. I will never be crushed by life's events.

---

[13] *Trusting God* (Colorado Springs: Navpress, 1989), P.21.

For a righteous man falls seven times, and rises again. But the wicked stumble in times of affliction (**Prov 24:16**).

It can be such a great hope to know that God controls all events in your life and that He will never allow you to be afflicted beyond what you can handle, even death. I know there may be times during heated arguments when you feel you can't handle it any more. But the truth is quoted in the verse below.

No temptation has overtaken you except such as is common to man; but God is faithful, who will not allow you to be tempted beyond what you are able, but with temptation will also make a way of escape, that you may be able to bear it (**1 Cor 10:13**).

Let's look at some practical and daily things you can do that will preserve hope when affliction comes your way

Practical Steps to Take During Affliction

When you have men like Steve and Mike living with difficult wives and them obviously living lives of sin, the mixture is filled with disaster. As for the reader, you may be going through some really hard times in your life due to all the problems that are occurring in your marriage. Let me give you some quick advise that I gave Steve and Mike as to how to live and survive daily with difficult wives.

Pray. This should be a very important aspect of your life, during and after affliction comes.[14]

***In return for my love they act as my accusers. But I am in prayer* (Psa 109:4).**

Your communion with God gauges your attitude and response to affliction in your life. I have found that if I'm far away from my personal fellowship with God, I'm more likely to respond sinfully and see hope dissipate from my attitude.

Meditate on God's Word. This is your second ingredient to responding properly to affliction. God's Word gives you hope by presenting principles for responding to affliction. It helps for you to sometimes understand why afflictions occur and how to handle them. By knowing these things, you have great hope amid all events in your life.

***This is my comfort in my affliction, that thy word has revived me* (Psa 119:50).**

What a great hope you have in God's Word!

Repent of any sins in your life. Confession of your sins is crucial to having a constant hope in all afflictions. Affliction will make you aware of your sin, and it brings you to repentance often.

---

[14] Read Dick Eastman, *The hour that changes the word.* Grand Rapids: Baker Book House, 1978.

Thou didst forgive the iniquity of thy people; Thou didst cover all their sin. Thou didst withdraw all thy fury; Thou didst turn away from thy burning anger **(Psa 85:2-4).**

God is a God of compassion and forgiveness. Your communion with Him is sweeter when you recognize and repent of any sins in your life. Through this action, hope is kindled. Take time to think about your life and how it compares to Biblical standards.

Hope in God and praise Him no matter what happens. Do not let circumstances dictate your response to life. Let Biblical truth saturate your life in such a way that over time you can delight in a thankful attitude, even praising God for His faithfulness toward you.

But I will hope continually, and I will praise you yet more and More…. Oh, do not let the afflicted return ashamed! Let the poor and needy praise your name **(Psa 71:14; 74:21b).**

Ask God to reveal to you any ways or desires you may have that could bring on afflictions.

Search me oh God, and know my heart; try me, and know my anxieties; and see if there is any wicked way in me, and lead me in the everlasting way **(Psa 139:23-24).**

Be honest with looking into your motives and heart. Find out why, in certain issues you actually choose to sin. There is a reason you choose to sin rather than obey God. It may be sensual pleasure, greed, fear of your reputation to others, etc. As a Christian God must be first above all these things.

Realize that God brings both good and bad into our lives for our blessing and His glory. We must accept both as God's loving providence, and in this so doing maintain hope.

Consider the work of God. For who can make straight what He has made crooked? In the day of prosperity be joyful, but in the day of affliction consider: surely God has appointed the one as well as the other (**Eccles 7:13-14**).

So no matter what state you're in, you can have hope that God knows what He is doing and you can still be thankful. Amen!

APPENDIX #1

Church Leaders In The Heat Of The Battle

This book was written for laymen who work at a job and come home to a situation that is not too friendly. For them it is almost like going into enemy territory, being ready to do battle. The Biblical plans I laid out, though, are true for those in church leadership also. But there is a drastic difference for those in leadership. When I originally wrote this book, it never dawned on me that these issues also affect church leaders. Then the Lord brought into my office two different pastors who were in the heat of these battles also. Let me give you two real-life counseling situations.

The first is a fellow I'll call "Pastor Confused" (I'll use "C" for his name). C was a very nice young man, married with two kids. He had been to a Christian college getting his Bible degree, and now had only a few classes left in seminary to earn his MDiv. degree. He was the family pastor at a large church and was very good at it. But when he came to me he was at first very inhibited and tended to beat around the bush, wasting time. I finally stopped him and asked him to be open and honest with me about what was really happening.

After pausing for a few minutes, with tears in his eyes, he finally opened up.

He had been the family pastor for about five years and he loved the position. But he said for all this time he had been hiding the truth from everyone at church, even the senior pastor. I was the first to hear this.

He had a terrible marriage. Their were continual arguments, yelling, threats, and his wife saying she hated him and was eventually going to divorce him. Now take a few moments and ponder this. Here was a family pastor ministering to many other families, working with them on similar situations yet his own marriage was in shambles. Not only had he done much over those past five years to hide his sins and put forth to others a façade, but he had been portraying to the church that everything was fine at home.

Many things ran through my mind as he spoke, things like "what a hypocritical man, what is he doing in the ministry?" I decided to be patient and let him spell out the truth. After about fifteen minutes, he finally finished and looked up at me and asked, *"What should I do?"* The answer was simple and clear but very difficult to give, because I knew the consequences would be dramatic. The answer I would give would be Biblical, not my own personal opinion. Yet, I felt very sorry for him because I know his situation is very common in many churches, most men are just very good at hiding it, like Pastor C. You may see your church leaders on Sunday with smiles, but after years of counseling I know many a church leader who had bad marriages but are stuck in them for the same reason as C. Think about this. Here sitting in front of me was a man who had just spent nine years of his life in intense schooling and training to be a pastor. He had invested five years into being a family pastor. Most of his adult life had consisted of pursuing this dream, and yet here he sat asking me, "what should I do?"

With a deep breath and an aching heart, I knew I had to tell him the truth. This is basically what I told him. *Pastor C, you have been living a hypocritical life toward your wife, children, all the people you minister to, and your senior pastor. For all these years you have been pretending that everything was fine in your home and portraying that to others. But all the while your own home has been falling apart and in no way a godly example to others. Pastor C, you need to go to your senior pastor and tell him the truth, then step down from the ministry. You also need to go to your small congregation and share with them the truth on your last Sunday. There are probably others in that small group who are doing what you've been doing, and this could help them as well toward being open and honest. Then you need to focus on your own marriage. This is now your ministry, saving your home from destruction. For years your wife has been living with and seeing a hypocrite. What she needs to see is a man who has true integrity and love toward his own family, thus showing forth an honest walk before the Lord. After stepping down, you need to get a non-ministry job to support your family.*

There is nothing worst to me than seeing men in leadership living the kind of lifestyle Pastor C had been living. I paused to see what his reaction would be. I knew this was a huge thing for him. Leaving behind all those years he had invested and starting afresh on a new career would not be easy. Then he said I was right and he would do this. He also said he knew this all the time, but the actual idea of doing what was right was too hard. It was easier to suppress the truth in his own heart and continue on in the ministry than to take the hard road to leaving full-time ministry and fixing his marriage.

I went on to share with him that his home situation is usually not something that can be fixed overnight. It took years of neglect and ungodly behavior to get him at this point in his marriage, and it may take many more years to bring his family to where it needs to be.

I also shared that the priority is not being in the ministry full-time; instead it is glorifying God in his marriage and as a godly father to his kids. God does not need him to succeed in bringing about the kingdom. What He wants are men of integrity, men who are honest examples of godliness before their families. God will not bless those who are living a facade in ministry, as Pastor C had been. Human effort will bring some results, but give me a man who is Biblically qualified as an elder and then you will see God within his midst. Confronting pastor's with the reality of their sinful life situations is probably the hardest counseling issue for me to do. For years they have been hiding the truth, and now with it exposed they usually sit dazed, realizing that God finally revealed their hidden secrets just as He said he would.

But if you will not do so, behold, you have sinned against the Lord, and be sure your sin will find you out (Num 32:23).

As they walk out of my office, I watch them and know that the long journey they are stepping into will do several things for the best. First, God will be glorified. Second, he will eventually learn more through the next several years about integrity, affliction, godliness and what true love really is than he could ever learn from a seminary class. This is not something you can read about in a book, it is applying God's Word to every-day life situations that grow and stretch them into a man of God, ready and equipped to minister.

My second example is one with not so happy an ending. I'll call him "Pastor Angry." His wife also had been living with a hypocrite for many years and had spent many a nights crying alone, raising the children by herself with her husband out "ministering." This second example came to my attention when this pastor's wife called me to discuss her husband's ministry and the problems they were having. She truly loved her husband and wanted to help him. As she shared what was going on, what I heard was a hurting wife. He was acting very rudely with her, was constantly yelling at her, ignoring her most of the time, and treating her as though she was always getting in the way of his success. He was counseling other people in marriage problems, preaching a series on Sundays on the family, and all the while his own marriage was in shambles. He was an angry man who had basically written off his wife as a meddler and one who was blocking his way to ministry greatness.

After she shared all this, I asked if we could all meet together and talk about this. She said her husband would not do this because he thought he was not the problem, she was. And if he did come, it would appear there was a problem and he didn't want others to know. A counseling professor and former pastor once told me that over the years one of the biggest problems he had seen for those in the ministry was their lack of ability to be open and honest with others about the problems they were having. Those in any type of church leadership are people too. They have their struggles, their hurts and pains, but if they share that with others the consequences are usually great. They could lose their jobs or be asked to step down from their leadership roles. So most leaders hide their problems and minister in a hypocritical state until God finally exposes things in the right manner, at the right time. This is why men in leadership must truly be Biblically qualified as elders before they enter the ministry. A simple Bible degree is not the answer. Time spent being Biblically qualified as an elder is the proving ground. It is here a tested, godly man can truly minister to others. The lay person sitting in the pew is asked to pursue Christ-likeness in the home, at work, and in their private lives. The qualified elder teaching then truly needs to be that godly leader, shepherding them in all honesty, integrity, transparency of their home and with a sincere heart and life.

I listened carefully to Pastor Angry's wife and at the end she asked me what they should do. I paused a minute and with a deep breath told her what Biblically needs to happen. I shared with her the Scriptures about what it means to be Biblically qualified as an elder at church and in the home. When I finished, the answer was quite clear. He was not qualified and she knew it. But what she said next surprised me. She said that even though I was right, she could not tell this to her husband. He had been doing this for many years, and to step down now would be too much of a life change for him and her. Furthermore, she said their two kids would be ashamed of their father.

I reiterated my stance but to no avail. Her love for her husband superseded her love for truth and integrity in the Lord. I gave her my email address and asked that she let me know what happened in the future. After hanging up, I felt this real emptiness and helplessness inside, as though at first I had failed. Here was a pastor living a terribly hypocritical ministry toward others and treating his own wife very badly. And to make things worse, she was covering up for his own sinful behavior toward her, the church members, and the Lord. But then my picture of the situation was enlarged and I realized that eventually God would expose Pastor Angry's sin and things would come crashing down on him. Not that I would feel better when this happens.

It's so sad to see a couple choose the harder path of affliction rather than doing the path of obedience. But I've seen it over and over again. It is sad that after God has confronted people with their sins through others in a very patient and loving way, He has to use affliction to some degree to bring them to repentance and open their eyes to the truth about themselves and their sins. I haven't heard from Pastor Angry's wife yet, but I do expect something from her in the future. God loves His church and will not let things like this go on. He will expose the truth about this man and in no way let him continue indefinitely in this hypocritical lifestyle.

Let's look now at what the actual qualifications are for a man desiring to go into ministry.

QUALIFICATIONS OF CHURCH LEADERSHIP

Church leadership is a very serious thing to God, and He has already laid out its criteria for us in the Scriptures. He wants those in leadership to be godly examples to His flocks, teaching them by an honest example of what it truly means to be a godly father, husband and Christian in all aspects of life. It has been my experience throughout my forty years as a Christian that those in these leadership positions are rare and very narrow for the truly qualified man of God. I've met thousands of pastors and have spoken in hundreds of churches in my lifetime, and one thing I have seen is that many are *"called"* but few are truly chosen. I could honestly say that most of the men I've have met in the ministry were not Biblically qualified, but they remained in the pastorate because that's all they ever knew how to do and to do something else would be unthinkable. There have been few among the many leaders I have known who would match up to these qualifications God has laid out. Why? Is it because they are too high for the average man to reach? No! God has made it attainable, but only to those who are qualified and truly chosen. When I come across a man who is actually Biblically qualified to be a pastor, he stands out like a jewel among many plain rocks. His high integrity, sound doctrine, good marriage and home life, all are open before others to see. There is no hiding of sins, instead an honest transparency that delights the soul and stands as an example to other men and families as to where they need to go spiritually.

Qualifications of Elders

The function of elders is clear Biblically. They are to teach and govern the local flock God has given them. They are doctrinal guardians and overseers of the lives of His flock. When it comes to the qualifications of an elder/pastor, they are summed up well in 1 Timothy 3:1-7.

3:1 "This is a faithful saying: If a man desires the position of an overseer [elder], he desires a good work."
Desires (oregetai/epithumei)

In order for a man (not a woman) to become an elder, God must prompt his heart, by God the Spirit to desire that high and very responsible position. It brings dishonor to God and the church for any man to enter this high calling for motives such as wealth, fame and other selfish reasons (1 Pet 5:1-3). This desire God puts within a man must then be carefully guarded by that man. If he knows he has been selected by God to full-time ministry, he must then set his course in life as to his purity, sound doctrinal training from a Biblically based school, and surround himself with other godly men. Lastly, but very important, he must prayerfully and wisely choose his wife, as God permits. The wife can either make or break his future ministry. I have lost count of how many men I have known who said they were called into the ministry during college or seminary but are not today. Why not? Because of an immoral relationship with their wives before marriage, impurity, and a lack of integrity before they got married. Fornication with one's future wife before marriage causes many problems after marriage and shows forth the man's lack of self control and discipline, and a low view of God's high calling.

3:2 *"An elder then must be blameless"*
Blameless (anepilempton)

This Greek word denoted living a life that gave no reasons for others within a man's own family or outside to think badly about him. (There will always be others who find reasons to mock pastors, but it should be because he stands for the truth, not because he is living a hypocritical life). It is here the elder's reputation is also at stake. How does he live with his wife, his children, among those within his sphere of influence? With our first example of "Pastor C", his reputation was heavily marred, he was living a hypocritical lifestyle; one way with his wife and another among his flock. A truly qualified elder can be open and honest about his relationships and the integrity of his life is excellent. Also, the focal point of this term is not on a person's relationship to the Lord, but on how others view his lifestyle. If you are a pastor reading this, be honest about your home life, your marriage, and your children. Can you be blamed for things in your relationships that should not be so? (Ps 101:6; Phil 3:17; 2 Thess 3:9; Heb 13:7; 1 Pet 5:3).

3:2 "The husband of one wife"
One women's husband (mias gunaikas andras)

The way this is written in the Greek, the emphasis is on *"one."* The point is not about whether or not an elder should be married, single, or divorced. The main issue is not the elder's marital status, but his moral and sexual purity. A "one-woman man" is clearly an elder who, if married, is totally devoted to his wife, maintaining singular devotion only to her and no other women, having affections and sexual purity toward her in both thoughts and deeds. To violate this is to forfeit blamelessness and being "above reproach" (Prov 6:32-33; Titus 1:6-7). This issue of being a one-woman man also has to do also with lust. Watch a man's eyes and see where they go, and you can sometimes peer into his heart. The gazes at other women show forth, even for a pastor, his true intentions. I am not saying he can't look at and talk to other women, that would be extreme. What I'm talking about is how he looks at other women, or maybe even other men! If an elder is truly qualified, you will see a man who has settled in his heart already that God has given him his wife. He knows it is both dishonoring to the Lord and a waste of time to lust after other women, since it would be destructive to pursue them any further.

A well-known pastor of a very large church in Southern California had a long -standing ministry, had written many fine Christian books, taught at a Christian university, and had a radio ministry. Best of all he had a lovely wife with several children. After thirty years of productive ministry, God finally exposed the pastor's adulterous relationship with his secretary. The repercussions of this exposure were huge. His wife divorced him, his kids were ashamed, he was fired from his church, and his whole life was discredited. Another young man I personally knew at my church was very intelligent, had a very fruitful ministry, a beautiful wife and child, and appeared to have a bright future as a pastor-that is until he was caught in an adulteress relationship with a young high school girl. Today he is a salesman back east. A life calling destroyed and for what? A temporary fix, a short fling, or some other trick of Satan. This calling must be taken seriously because God is a serious God when it comes to those in leadership positions.

3:2 "Temperate"
Temperate (nephalion)

This particular word is used twice in the New Testament-here in 1 Timothy 3:11 of the women (wives of) deacons, and in Titus 2:2 about the older men in the church. The word carries the idea of self-control or mastery over one's desires. The basic root meaning is "wineless," but it is here used metaphorically to mean "alert, watchful, vigilant, or clear headed." Qualified elders must be able to think clearly. Hopefully, the man called into the ministry will think this way concerning both his purity of life and soundness of doctrine. Truly qualified leaders are disciplined men who have mastered their desires. As Paul said, *"I will not be mastered by anything"* (1 Cor 6:12).

3:2 "Sober-minded"
Sober-minded, sensible, prudent, reasonable (**Sophrona**)

The Greek word used here is also used in Titus 1:8 and 2:2 of older men and 2:5 of younger women. A sober-minded man is disciplined, knows how to properly place his priorities of life, and is a man who is serious about his spiritual responsibilities, not only for himself but for his family and flock. He is able to discern well, to see things as they really are with all their problems, social issues, and most of all Biblical truth in a world of deceiving lies. This kind of elder doesn't go with the flow of society, culture, or whimsical ways of teachings. Instead he is able to speak and live out Biblical truth and be that example to his family and flock of how a true Christian should live, act and speak.

3:2 "Of good behavior"
Good behavior, respectable, honorable (**Kosmios**)

The Greek word means "orderly." The elder's life must not be chaotic or confused, either at home or in the church. If his life is chaotic, how could he ever lead the flock toward Christ-likeness? Never! There are many believers within the church whose lives may be chaotic, not knowing from one hour to the next what's going to happen with their lives, but not so with the elders. Their paths are well worn. They are the kind of people who are predictable because their lives are orderly, godly, well thought out. If variations or afflictions come their way, they will handle them Biblically. There are no hidden sins, either in his family life or in the church. His good behavior is just the fruit of a pure heart before the Lord. Does this then mean he is perfect? Of course not! But he is repentant from a pure heart and greatly desires Christ-likeness.

3:2 "Hospitable"
Hospitable (philoxenon)

This Greek word is a compound term meaning a "lover of strangers" (Rom 12:13; Heb 13:2; 1 Pet 4:9). As with all the spiritual virtues, an elder is to have his home and life open for all to observe, and as an example of what a godly home should be like for those strangers and those of his flock. An elder in ministry who has a bad marriage will have to hide his home life from others, because if exposed it will bring the loss of his job. What a terrible way to live.

3:2 "Able to teach"
Skilled in teaching (didaktikon).

This Greek word is used only here and in 2 Timothy 2:24. This qualification is the one that sets deacons and elders apart. This is the primary duty of an elder, the preaching/teaching of God's Word and the living out of those principles before others (1 Tim 4:6,11,13;5:17; 2 Tim 2:15, 24; Titus 2:1). He must be able to give sound, Biblical instructions and counseling to his flock, setting a good example in his everyday walk among family, friends and associates, and be able to refute those who seek to contradict the truth. The more he teaches the Word of God, the more he will find the need to refute cult teachings outside the church and well-hidden contradictions within the church. This is why he must know Biblical doctrine well and be able to stand strong, yet humble, to explain truth to people. He must be astute enough theologically to discern serious errors and teach the truth from God's word. But let me emphasize something here. I've known many good teachers in the pulpit whose family life was terrible. To be a qualified elder both teaching and life at home must be God glorifying, never a contradiction.

3:3 *"not given to wine"*
Not addicted to wine (me paroinon)

This is more than a prohibition against drunkenness (Eph 5:18). A qualified elder must not have a reputation as a drinker, his judgment must never be clouded by alcohol (Prov 31:4, 5; 1 Cor 6:12). His personal life at home, in the community and at church must be radically different from the world, and it should lead all toward holiness rather than compromising toward sin. He should not lead a life to see how close he can get to sin without sinning, but should be striving toward Christ-likeness and holiness. He must look at himself, his speech, his lifestyle, and his family life and honestly see how he can do things that please his savior. His testimony is just as important as everything else.

3:3 *"Not violent"*
Not violent, belligerent or pugnacious (me plekten)

The actual Greek says, "Not a giver of blows." The world's ways are easy- get revenge, fight back, protect your rights, gossip, hit others if you can to hurt them. But Christians are to be radically different, as Jesus pointed out on the Sermon on the Mount in Matthew 5-7. Elders, likewise, being the example to others in the flock and at home, are to react differently in difficult situations. They are to act calmly and gently, showing forth a whole different response to a hostile world (2 Tim 2:24-25).

An elder must not be an angry man who uses violent words or fists to solve his problems. Instead he actually puts other persons first in helping them before himself. He must be under control and well disciplined. A pastor who gets angry because he can't get his way is a man who needs to change.

3:3 "But gentle"
Gentle (epieke)

This kind of man should be a man of extreme gentleness- *power under control.* He is not a sickly, passive man, but strong in gentleness, knowing how to take a lot of heat without getting angry. With great discernment he speaks the right words and takes the right actions. His goal in a difficult situation is not revenge, hate or hitting, instead bringing peace to difficult circumstances. His character should be one that is well known for gentleness.

This quality is mentioned again after "not a lover of money." It is "peaceable" (*amachon*). This word carries great implications about how an elder speaks and uses words. He is not only considerate, but congenial, gracious in words-not from phoniness, but from a heart that seeks purity of thought, motives and deeds. He is quick to pardon a wrong and one who does not hold a grudge. After all, is it not the meek who will inherent the earth?

3:3 "Not greedy for money"
Not a lover of money (aphilarguron)

His goal in life is not to become rich or of having a reputation for hoarding things. His primary goal as an elder is the Kingdom of God, which is not of this world. This physical world, all its money, banks, cars, homes, and wealth are all going to be melted away one day (2 Pet 3:10-11). Therefore the elder's passion is to do the work of God on this disposable planet, sharing the gospel, living a life that is an example to others of holiness, showing his own family the way of Christ in all his actions, words, and motives. He uses money as a good steward uses a gift from God to meet his family's needs, helping the poor, giving to other ministries, and glorifying God. He should not be so money-oriented that it affects his ministry decisions or testimony before his family or flock (Tit 1:7; 1 Pet 5:2).

Any leader, pastor or teacher whose in the ministry for wealth eventually reveals his true motivations, and that is usually through his own family who knows him most intimately at home. This kind of man has his heart set on the temporary world and not on the kingdom (Matt 6:24; 1 John 2:15). False teachers within the church are usually characterized by this quality of greed (Titus 1:11; 2 Pet 2:1-3; 14; Jude 11). In counseling I've noticed that in many situations the greed for *money* and *things* is at the core of marital conflicts. The truly qualified elder has set aside his right to have anything in this world, but sees it all as God's. If God grants him anything he delightfully uses it as a good steward toward the right things. Paul the apostle was a man well educated, standing above his own peers mentally, and was well respected. Yet, after becoming a Christian, he could say the following:

But what things were gain to me, these I have counted loss for Christ. Yet indeed also count all things loss for the excellence of the knowledge of Christ Jesus my Lord, for whom I have suffered loss of all things, and count them as rubbish (Phil 3:7-8).

Dear pastor, if you are in the ministry or feel called into it; let this be found in you, that all things in this world are only a temporary stewardship given by God for His kingdom. And if God grants you any kind of material blessings, which He may because of your long faithfulness, again, see them as God's and be thankful. But in no way seek after them. God will meet your needs.

3:3, "not quarrelsome"
Not quarrelsome (amachon)

He seeks peace as his goal, not winning arguments. He is reluctant to fight or argue, because his goal is to eventually bring unity and harmony among others. That is what the Kingdom of God in heaven and eventually on the new earth is like, and this is God's goal for an elder, even among a world filled with hate and disunity. In the church and at home his goal is peace and unity. At the same time he realizes there will always be those whose goal in life is fighting, quarreling and causing disunity. He must use discernment to know when to back off and let God take care of those stubborn fellows. Paul was a man who suffered much at the hands of violent men who hated the gospel, yet he could say, *"If it is possible, as much as depends on you, live peaceably with all men. Beloved, do not avenge yourselves, but rather give place to wrath: for it is written,*

"Vengeance is Mine, I will repay," says the Lord. Therefore "if your enemy is hungry, feed him; If thirsty, give him a drink; for in doing you will heap coals of fire on his head" (Rom. 12:18-20). The elder though must also realize that his is a position of guardianship of the truth and must defend it against all those who want to twist the truth for their own benefit. In these situations, with all humbleness, he protects the truth and exposes error.

3:4-5 *"one who manages his own household well, having his children in submission with all reverence (for if a man does not know how to rule his own house, how will he take care of the church of God?) Leader of a well-ordered household* (kalos proistamenon).

Here we meet the crux of the issues. A man's home, not the pulpit, will reveal his true character. A well-trained and educated seminarian may be a great teacher in the pulpit and well admired in the church, but his marriage may be terrible, his children lost and unruly, and his stewardship of God's resources in disorder. Yet, he appears to be in control. Our two true-life pastoral examples at the beginning of this section show that this problem is not rare but common. I have lost count of how many elders/pastors I've known whose practice did not match up to their qualifications. The home is truly the proving ground for a man's qualifications as an elder. The elder's personal and home life must be exemplary. He must rule over (preside over, have authority over) his home well and see it as a stewardship given by God. He will one day give an account to God for how he ruled, whether it was with gentleness, forgiveness, love, and seeing others as more important than himself. The word "*submission*" here is a military term referring to soldiers ranked under one in authority. Also, an elder's children must be believers, well behaved and respectful (Titus 1:6). His wife should be respected and tenderly loved, even sacrificially. Their personal relationship should be openly admirable and transparent, an example of how a Christian marriage should be.

3:7 "not a novice, lest being puffed up with pride he fall into the same condemnation as the devil" A mature believer, not a new convert **(me neophuton)**

Elders are to be men who have proven themselves over time within the church to have been faithful and discerning men, good husbands and fathers, ones with a good reputation and theologically sound. They are not to be new converts (5:22). Satan's condemnation spoken of here was one of pride over his position (Prov 16:18; Isa 14:12-14; Ezek 28:11-19). This same kind of sin can happen much easier to a newer convert than to an experienced and proven man of God. A new believer, even though having charisma and good talking abilities, may fall into prideful situations and lead many astray. Part of the elder's seasoning is a humbling process along with the practice of Biblical principles over the years in marriage and the raising of children and dealings with others.

3:7 "Moreover he must have a good testimony among those who are outsiders, lest he fall into reproach and the snare of the devil" Good reputation with outsiders **(Marturian Kalen)**

This is very similar to verse 2 where Paul says the elder must be "blameless." But here it is explicit that even the lost, the "outsiders," unbelieving world, respect him and can put no realistic blame on him. This doesn't mean he has compromised the Word of God so much that he no longer stands for the truth against a hostile world. The qualified elder is one who has an impeachable reputation within the unbelieving community, even though those people disagree with his moral and theological stands (Matt 5:48; Phil 2:15).

But the verse goes on to say, *"lest he fall into the reproach and snare of the devil."* This is also referred to in 2 Timothy 2:26. It appears to involve deception and sin that the lost have caught him in, even though those within the church have been blinded by the fact he was just a very good actor. Here we have come full circle. It started with the elder's inner qualifications, moved to his behavior within his home and flock, and now even his reputation with the lost. The well-qualified elder's whole life is put on trial here by Paul to show forth the high calling of God for such men. His inner life, family life, and life to the world are to be such that people see integrity, holiness, seriousness, godliness and sound teaching from God's Word.

I'll never forget the true story of a very famous evangelist who was well known around the world. He held crusades with huge crowds and had written many Christian books and songs. The church didn't know, however, that he lived a second, hidden life. Eventually the world press and law caught up to his sinful lifestyle and all was exposed. Pornography, prostitution, drinking, and misuse of much money were brought to light. That brought his ministry and reputation to a halt and heaped shame on Christ. Even today there is shame when his name is mentioned, especially to the "outsiders."

This list I have gone over is not exhaustive. Timothy and Titus use different words to describe the same qualifications. Hopefully the point is clear that the qualifications are high, as is the calling, responsibilities, and accountability before God. No man should aspire to be an elder or, worse, remain an elder until he gets these things right in his own life and practices them over a period of time. If you are presently a pastor and have honestly found yourself not qualified, here is my Biblical counsel: Do the right thing! Go to your leaders and explain to them honestly and openly your situation, then step down from the ministry. It is here that you will truly find peace of soul and yet realize that the road you have chosen will not be an easy one. Set your sites on doing things God's way. Then, find a decent job in which you can support your family and aspire to meet these qualifications as an elder or deacon.

As Christians, Christ is our example, and that example is not only laid out for us in the four Gospels, it is categorically laid out for us here in 1Timothy 3. Our goal is to be at the very least deacon-qualified. (As I said earlier, the only difference between an elder and deacon is the teaching gifts.) If you make this radical change then you are on your way to pleasing the Lord. But if you continue to hide your problems, your marriage and sins, God will eventually expose them for what they are. Then the exposure will be shameful instead of honorable. If you are a leader and realize that you are not qualified as an elder, you must also ask yourself the next difficult question, "Am I really a Christian?" Maybe you've acted religious all your life but you're not born again (John 3). Look at the following test and be honest and answer the questions concerning your real faith. It is between you and God.

APPENDIX 2

The Faith Test

People from all over the world, in all kinds of faiths, claim to have some kind of spirit, either within or from without, guiding and empowering them to do certain things in this life. The issue for true believers is "Am I truly a Christian?" Scripture is clear; if you are not born again, you're simply not truly saved, maybe just very religious. But religion will not get you to eternity with God. Hell is full of religious people. In fact, everyone there is now very religious. They know for certain that God does exist and that His Word is true. Only now it's too late for them. But for the reader of this book, his or her judgment hasn't come yet. As one looks at his life and asks this all important question, there will be two major evidences: First, to either prove one is saved or second, to show forth one's heart as maybe religious but lost. The first will be the internal evidence of the Spirit's work of sanctification. The second will be the external evidence in one's behavior brought about by the internal change of regeneration by the indwelling Spirit. Let's look at the internal evidence first. Take the test below and see how you do.

Internal Evidences Tested

Take some time and read the book of 1 John. Then answer the following questions honestly, searching your heart for the truth about your relationship with the Lord. Answer either yes or no.

a. I have a deep desire to worship God:_____.

b. I love to commune with the Father daily in prayer:_____.

c. I look forward to reading God's Word and seeing how He wants me to think and live:_____.

d. I am very serious about my sin and seek to apply God's Word to it in order to change and practice His ways daily:_____.

e. I'm growing daily in my desire to be holy:_____.

f. I do not hate, but am growing to love others as God loves me, even though I rebel against Him at times:_____.

g. I desire more than anything to be Christ-like:_____.

h. I am willing to give up anything in following Christ:_____.

i. I am content:____.

j. I am honest:_____.

k. I am forgiving____.

l. I see others as more important than myself____.

Look up the following verses and write out what they teach:

Galatians 5:16

Ephesians 5:18

John 16:13

1 Thessalonians 5:19

Galatians 5:25

Ephesians 4:30

Hebrews 13:5

Romans 14:17-19

External Evidences Tested

Look at the following questions and see if there are external evidences that show the effects of that internal regeneration through the Holy Spirit. But keep in mind this very important principle. One's external evidences should be the fruit of the Holy Spirit's work internally, not externals only. Legalism and religion are exemplified by these external things alone.

1) I see a lessening of sinful behavior and more righteous behavior in my life:_____
2) The way I dress shows that I do not want to draw attention to myself but instead to have others see a difference in my life by godliness:____
3) My life is growing in practical discipline, cleanliness, and respectful observance of other people? ____

4) As the Holy Spirit works in my life, I see Him bringing order out of my chaotic lifestyle:_____. If not, what is it that is in disorder?

5) Ask three people who know you well the following question:

"Do you see my lifestyle as one that exemplifies Christ-? likeness?"

(Ask them to be honest and open toward you in their answer.)

First person's name _____

Relationship_____

Answer _____. Why?

Second person's name_____

Relationship_____

Answer _____. Why?

Third person's name_____

Relationship_____

Answer _____. Why?

6) People see me as more loving and forgiving toward others:_____.

7) I do not smoke and drink:_____.

8) I do not flirt with the opposite sex if I'm married:_____.

9) I am honest on my taxes:_____.

10) I work on my job as though Jesus were my boss:_____.

11) I treat everyone, no matter what race, color or religion, with respect and dignity:_____.

12) I do not use vulgar or cursing language:_____.

13) No one can blame me for something sinful:_____.

14) I enjoy the fellowship of other believers:_____.

15) I do not steal from work or business:_____.

16) I do not gossip about others:_____.

Look up the following verses and write out what they teach.

Titus 2:7

2 Thessalonians 3:7

1Timothy 3:2

1 Thessalonians 2:10

1Timothy 5:22

1 Thessalonians 3:7

Ephesians 4:2

Romans 12:17

1 Thessalonians 4:11-12

Matthew 5:44

1 Corinthians 9:25

Romans 14:1-23

Titus 2:14

Galatians 6:2

Acts 11:14, 30

Acts 2:42

1 Thessalonians 5:11

All of these internal desires and attributes will be in a truly born-again believer, and their ***external behavior will be the fruit of their new birth***. Men who have been regenerated by the Holy Spirit exhibit a new nature, new desires, and a new perspective on life. Instead of seeing the world as revolving around them (selfishness), they now see things the way Christ sees them. They are now *"other oriented."* All of these principles are found John 4 and 1 John. Read these texts and see how you truly measure up. The Spirit's goal is to bring the believer to Christ-likeness. Look up the following verses and write out what they teach about this issue of Christ-likeness.

2 Corinthians 3:18

2 Corinthians 5:14-17

Galatians 5:22-23

Romans 8:1-17

Philippians 3:20-21

Look at the following verses and see how important this issue is concerning the Spirit and salvation. There is a divine order among the Trinity, though each member is equal in power and glory. Thus there is an agreed-upon economy of their salvation work-election is by the eminency of the Father, reconciliation by the Son, and sanctification by the Spirit.

For those who continually live according to the flesh set their minds on the things of the flesh, but those who live according to the Spirit, the things of the Spirit **(Rom 8:5).**

For as many as are lead by the Spirit of God, these are sons of God **(Rom 8:14).**

Beloved, do not believe every spirit, but test the spirits, whether they are from God **(1 John 4:1).**

You are of God, little children, and have overcome them, because He [the Holy Spirit] who is in you is greater than he who is in the world [Satan] (1 John 4:4).

In this the children of God and the children of the devil are made plain: whoever does not continually practice righteousness is not of God, nor is he who does not love his brother (1 John 3:10).

These are sensual persons, who cause divisions, not having the Spirit (Jude 19).

It is clear that one who has the Spirit of God exhibits certain fruit in his life that proves he is truly saved and the Spirit indwells him. First John gives us a clear picture of how we can truly know we are saved and Spirit indwelt.

Now he who keeps His commandments abides in Him and He in him. And by this we know that He abides in us, by the Spirit whom He has given us (1 John 3:24).

How can we know we are saved and have the Spirit? There are several things in the above verses that can give one the assurance of his or her salvation.

WE BELIEVE THE GOSPEL

At conversion, God has given us His Spirit to dwell within because we believed the gospel. He regenerated us and gave us a new nature that can overcome sin and practice righteousness. Now we can't see the Holy Spirit because He is a spirit. Jesus said this in John 3 when He compared the Spirit to the wind. You can't see wind, only its effects. So it is with the believer and the presence of the Spirit—one should see the effects or fruits in one's life. In 1 John 4:14-15, the apostle says *"And we have seen and testify that the Father has sent the Son as Savior into the world. Whoever confesses that Jesus is the Son of God, God [Spirit], abides in him and he in God."* How does a person know he or she has the Spirit? Not by some feeling, visions, or the hearing of voices. Biblically you know you have the Spirit because you believe the facts- that the Father has sent the Son to be the Savior of the world and you have confessed that He is your only Savior. The actual belief in the gospel is thus evidence of the presence of the Spirit in one's life. Mankind, on their own, cannot know God.

But the natural man [lost] does not receive the things of the Spirit of God, for they are foolishness to him; nor can he know them because they are spiritually discerned (**1 Cor 2:14**).

WE HAVE THE LOVE OF GOD

A true believer comes to understand and believe that God gave believer's His Spirit because of His eternal love for them,*" And we have known and believed the love that God has for us."* God is love; His nature is one of love. But the verse goes on, *God is love, and he who abides in love abides in God and God [Spirit] in him"* (1 John 4:16). Inserted within this chapter is a doctrinal test to identify the true believer who has been given the Spirit.

a) You have to understand and believe God the Father and who He is.

b) You have to believe the Son and that He is God. That He is the Savior of the world, and that men need to be saved from their sin.

c) That by faith in Christ alone one comes to God for salvation.

The final test, according to verse 16, is that you *"love"* God and it shows in you're daily life. A true believer doesn't love the world system, but his or her love is for God, for others, and even enemies. This is the behavior/moral test. Every believer needs to look honestly into his own heart and see if these things are there.

Love is our confidence in judgment before God (1 John 4:17-18). Upon your conversion and the Spirit's coming to take up permanent residence within, the love of God is shed abroad in your heart. When that kind of perfected love is within you, you can have confidence on the Day of Judgment. First John 2:28 reads, *"And now little children [believers], abide in Him, that when He appears [Christ's second coming], we may have confidence and not be ashamed before Him at His coming."* For the true believer, there is no fear at this event, instead an expectation of hope. Because of the evidence of love in your life and obedience to His Word, you can go into the presence of God with boldness and confidence because all will be well!

The last statement in 1 John 4:17 is amazing. *"Because as He is, so are we in the world."* The Father will treat us the same way He treats the Son. As Jesus is, in the eyes of the Father, so God sees us. Because we have been covered in Christ's righteousness, we can stand before God as our loving and caring Father. First John

3:2 reads, *"Beloved, NOW we are children of God, and it has not yet been revealed what we shall be, but we know that when He is revealed, we shall be like Him, for we shall see Him as He is."*

While here on earth, we can't tell what we will be in perfection, but we will be like Him at His coming. For now we have been given God's love in our hearts, which superimposes itself over our old natures. Through regeneration this new love grows and matures (is perfected) as we grow in our devotion to God and obedience to His Word. If there is a lack of love for God and others, and fear in your life when Christ returns, it just might mean you're not a Christian at all.

WE HAVE A DESIRE TO WORSHIP

The Spirit helps us worship God (John 4:23-24). Only the born-again believer, one who has put his faith in Christ, can rightly worship God. Jesus made this very clear to the apostles and believers throughout history.

The true <u>worshippers</u> will worship the Father in <u>Spirit and truth</u>; for the Father is seeking such to worship Him **(John 4:23-24).**

It must also be mentioned that many around the world worship "God" or some other form of a god. Yet God has made a righteous path unto Himself through Christ the only Messiah. The road to hell is probably marked *"the religious way,"* yet it leads to destruction.

These people draw near to me with their mouth, and honor me with their lips, but their hearts are far from Me. And in

vain they worship Me, teaching as doctrines the command-
ments of men (**Matt 15:8-9**).

If one has no desire to worship God, then he or she must search
their heart to see if they are true believers. A Spirit-indwelt believer
will want to worship Him. In the above verse, Jesus was quoting
Isaiah 29:13. Through all of human history man has always been
motivated to create his own way to God. It started in Genesis 11
with the tower of Babel and continued in the land of Israel among
the delivered people of God. Jesus confronted man-directed worship
again during His ministry on earth, and it is still prevalent today.

WE HAVE A DESIRE TO PRAY

The Spirit gives us the right and ability to pray. Many people
in many different religions pray, but only those who are truly born-
again and have the Spirit dwelling within have the right and the
ability to pray and have those prayers answered by God. The arena in
which that occurs is tremendous. The Father in heaven is enthroned;
our advocate Christ (who is our divine lawyer, Heb. 4:14-16; 1 John
2:1), who is sitting at the right hand of the Father, pleads our prayers
before the Father; and the Spirit, who is our intercessor, pleads our
prayers before Christ. In this divine process, our prayers come before
God, who answers them, either yes, no, or wait. He always gives us
what is best for His purpose and our ultimate good. This part is
critical to true spiritual growth in one's life. Only a true believer has
a desire to pray and commune with God.

Praying always with all prayer and supplication in the
sphere of the Spirit (**Eph 6:18**).

Likewise the Spirit also helps us in our weakness. For we do not know what we should pray as we should, but the Spirit Himself makes intercession for us (**Rom 8:26-27**).

WE PERSEVERE

Therefore, my beloved brethren, be steadfast, immovable, always abounding in the work of the Lord, knowing that your labor is not in vain in the Lord (**1 Cor 15:58**).

One of the evidences that you have the Spirit is that you are still striving to be Christ-like, even after a period of rebellion and sin. A *"religious"* person goes on living a dual lifestyle: one of continual, habitual sinning, with little change toward Christ-likeness in his or her life, yet still believing in God (James 2:19). But the true believer, as he looks back over the years, sees spiritual growth. He can easily see the Spirit working and slowly guiding his life and growth toward being like Christ. Sometimes there is an awe and amazement to see all the things God has done within us. He has been faithful to continue the sanctification process when we were not all that faithful. Look up the following verses and write out what each teaches.

Ephesians 6:18

John 10:28-29

Romans 11:29

Philippians 1:6

1 Peter 1:5

Job 17:9

John 15:9

Acts 13:43

Romans 2:7

Galatians 6:9

2 Timothy 3:16

Hebrews 12:1

1 Peter 1:13

Revelation 3:11

Buy and read John MacArthur's book *Hard to Believe* (Nashville: Thomas Nelson, 2003).

APPENDIX 3

Three Ways To Glorify God In Your Life

What is the chief end of man? To glorify God! God is so great and merciful that we all should bow down on our knees and glorify Him for His great work of redemption.

Whoever offers praise glorifies Me; and to him who orders his conduct right, I will show the salvation of God (Psa 50:23).

When looking at the attributes of God and His awesome power and authority, one sees in them the reason we are to glorify Him—His attributes show forth to all creation His greatness. All the angels in heaven, all the saints and creatures before God's throne, fall down before Him and worship. Why do they do this? Because in heaven all sin and entanglements are removed and a clearer reality exists. There is an all-powerful awareness of whom and what God is- a reality, unseen by earthly eye, of God in all His attributes showing forth from the throne as lightening. We humans, encompassed by the fallen creation and our own sin, naturally resist bending the knee, due to pride and lack of love for God and His extreme mercy. But upon our salvation and the permanent indwelling of the Spirit, this alone gives us both the desire and ability to worship the Lord in all His deserved glory. Thus, the chief end, O Christian, is to seek to glorify God in all your thoughts, actions, and motives.

Look at the following verses and write out what each teaches about the glory of God.

1. John 15:8

2. 1 Peter 4:11

3. 1 Peter 4:14, 16

4. Psalm 50:15

5. Romans 15:9

6. 2 Corinthians 9:13

After doing this study, describe where and how you have glorified God in your life.

Now list the areas in your life where you have **not** glorified God.

The Scriptures teach that there are basically three ways we glorify God in our lives: upward toward Him, inward toward being Christ-like, and outward toward others in evangelism. As we are obedient to God's Word, through the power of the indwelling Spirit, practicing daily His principles out of a sincere love for Him, we are glorifying Him. This is the process of flushing out sin from our lives. Let's look at twenty Biblical principles for glorifying God in our lives. **Look up the following verses and write out how each applies to your life.**

UPWARD

1. Living to glorify God: 1 Corinthians 10:13.

2. Confessing your sins: Joshua 7.

1. Living a pure life: 1 Corinthians 6:18-20.

2. Submitting to Christ: Ephesians 5:24; Hebrews 12:9.

3. Praising God daily: 2 Corinthians 4:15.

4. Obeying God's Word: 2 Corinthians 9:13.

5. Giving to God for others: 2 Corinthians 9:6-15, 17.

6. Growing in Christ-likeness: Romans 4:20-21.

7. Suffering for God: 1 Peter 4:15-16.

8. Rejoice in God: 1 Chronicles 16:10.

9. Worshiping God: Psalm 86:9.

10. Bearing spiritual fruit: John 15:8.

13. Praying: John 14:13.

INWARD

1. Obeying God's Word: 2 Thessalonians 3:1; 1 Peter 10:1-11.

2. Keeping the church pure: Ephesians 5:27.

3. Helping to bring unity: John 17:22.

OUTWARD

1. Evangelizing others: Psalm 21:5, Ephesians 1:6, 12, and 14.

2. Showing forth the transformed life: Matthew 5:16.

3. Spreading the gospel: 2 Corinthians 12:14.

4. Walking by the Spirit: Galatians 5:16-25.

According to these verses, what is our chief end? Psalm 72:18-19; Philippians 4:20.

Looking at your life, is it purpose-driven to glorify God?

What *"things"* are in the way? Be honest and list below.

Buy and read John MacArthur's book, <u>*The Keys to Spiritual Growth*</u> (Wheaton, Ill.: Crossway Books, 2001).

Now go to your accountability person and share your results with them. Also, seek God in prayer daily about those areas of your life that don't glorify God.

RESOURCES FOR FURTHER RESEARCH & STUDY

*T*hese resources are listed because they could be key books in helping you deal with issues in your life and applying the Word of God, through the power of the Spirit, to those issues.

Jay Adams, *The Christian Counselor's Manual.* Presbyterian & Reformed Publishing Co., Phillipsburg, New Jersey, 1973.

Mike Cleveland, *Pure Freedom: Breaking the Addiction to Pornography.* Bemidji, Minn., Focus Publishing, 2002.

Dr. Wayne Mack and Joshua Mack, *The Fear Factor.* Hensley Pub. Tulsa, Oklahoma, 2002.

Martha Peace, *The Excellent Wife.* Focus Publishing, Bemidji, Minn., 1995.

Dr. Stuart Scott, *The Exemplary Husband.* Focus Publishing Co. Bemidji, Minn., 2002

Dr. Robert Smith, *The Christian Counselor's Medical Desk Reference.* Timeless texts, Stanley, North Carolina, 2000.

Dr. Edward T. Welch, *Blame It on the Brain.* R & R Publishing. Phillipsburg, New Jersey, 1998.

Printed in the United States
118994LV00002BA/257/P

9 781606 470718